life

Living in Fulfillment
Every Day

Annemarie Greenwood
and Marissa Campbell

iUniverse, Inc.
Bloomington

iUniverse books may be ordered through booksellers or by contacting:

iUniverse
1663 Liberty Drive
Bloomington, IN 47403
www.iuniverse.com
1-800-Authors (1-800-288-4677)

ISBN: 978-1-4620-6953-8 (sc)
ISBN: 978-1-4620-6955-2 (hc)
ISBN: 978-1-4620-6954-5 (e)

Printed in the United States of America

iUniverse rev. date: 1/12/2012

To Gary, Tyler and Amber with love.
To Dave, Lochlin, Aidan and Brendan with love.
Thank you for your patience, unconditional
love and unwavering support.
This book is also dedicated to anyone who desires
a life of happiness and fulfillment.
In gratitude,
Annemarie & Marissa

Contents

Acknowledgments

We would like to acknowledge and thank the wonderful people who, with their love and compassion, have helped guide us along our journeys. We would also like to express our gratitude toward the many incredible teachers in our lives who have helped shape and mold our philosophies and our experiences with their challenging lessons and obstacles. You have each contributed to this book in unique and profound ways. Thank you.

We thank our families and relatives; our friends, old and new; our yoga students; our teachers and guides; and the universe for allowing us to be the conduit for this significant message.

We would also like to extend a special *thank you* to Amber for her elegant book design and to our editors Norine, Teri, Erni, Gabrielle and Tonya. Your creativity, insight and keen eyes were instrumental in helping bring this book to fruition.

In gratitude,
Annemarie & Marissa

Introduction

Are you living your potential in this life? Are you truly fulfilled? Or are you left wanting, wondering what is missing? Many people will search throughout their existence, trying to find lasting happiness and peace, but do they really know what they are looking for? They find moments of peace and joy but then slip effortlessly back under the veil of unhappiness and struggle. Happiness is your birthright, and your sole purpose in this life is to be happy and fulfilled.

By removing the obstacles that have held you back and embracing a philosophy that is rooted in the simple message of following what feels good, you begin to transform your experience. You begin to examine everything you think, say and do, thereby discovering how to manifest a full and meaningful life.

LIFE: Living in Fulfillment Every Day was written as a guide to help you find your own unique path to happiness and fulfillment. Its format is distinctly unconventional compared with other self-help books in that we reveal the knowledge and tools necessary to live in fulfillment and happiness every day through the dynamic expression of a spiritual discourse. Grace, an enlightened teacher, guides Eve, an unfulfilled woman, on a journey of self-discovery and personal growth. The two women meet and spend a transformative day at the beach. Under the brilliant blue sky, amongst the sights and sounds of a small lakeside resort, they explore the path to *LIFE: Living in Fulfillment Every Day.*

Through detailed explanations, visualization exercises and thorough descriptions, Grace gently guides Eve toward self-awareness and empowerment. Through Grace's completely accessible teachings and powerful message, like Eve, you too may experience an awakened sense of purpose, compelling you to make the powerful decision to live an authentic life, one where you no longer compromise your happiness and you live each moment with passion, joy and absolute delight.

We are both registered yoga teachers and spend our lives helping and teaching others to find peace of mind and well-being. Our combined interest in and experience with yoga's philosophy and teachings span over six decades, but the knowledge to write this book did not come from reading ancient texts. *LIFE: Living in Fulfillment Every Day* was created using the yogic concept of *Svadyaya*, which is Sanskrit for "self-study" and "reflection," and the Buddha's guiding principle to not accept anything at face value—just because someone or something says so—but rather, observe, experience and analyze concepts to determine if they are true. Our everyday circumstances and ruminations provided the catalyst and experiential knowledge for writing this book. It is our sincere hope that the message in these pages resonates deeply within you and that it awakens a new way of seeing your life and the world around you, empowering you to find your truth, embody your fullest potential and live the life you've always wanted!

In gratitude,

Annemarie & Marissa

Chapter 1

An Unprecedented Encounter

Eve stood looking out over the lightening water. The sun was just beneath the horizon, and the mist floated serenely above the lake's surface. She sighed. It was the last day of her vacation, and she wasn't in any real hurry to get back. After nothing but sun, sand and water, she felt a real reluctance about saying good-bye to the beach and the summer. It had been a wonderful vacation, though, and she didn't really understand the feeling of melancholy that was settling deep within her bones. It's not as if she thought the vacation could last forever. No, that wasn't it. It was a disappointment of sorts, she assumed, but disappointment about what?

She considered the job she was returning to but waved that away with an imaginary hand. She liked her job—well, most of it anyway. Despite some minor tension with a co-worker, she loved what she was doing and really enjoyed interacting with the customers.

She felt anticipatory strain about getting the kids ready and off to school, but she was grateful that they seemed happy, or at least resigned, about their impending fate. She'd had a wonderful time with her husband, holding hands as they walked along the beach, kids splashing through the waves beside them. They even stole furtive kisses now and then as they sat side by side, soaking up the sun's glorious rays. She even had a tan, which was nothing short of miraculous, given her very pale skin tone. She had light blonde hair and grey-blue eyes and had always been wary of tarrying too long in the sun. But this week she had thrown caution to the wind—well, as much as could be considered daring while armed with SPF 60—and had managed to acquire a respectably healthy glow.

She shook her head in confusion. No, she was happy with everything in her life, yet she could not deny the downward pull stirring from deep within, though she couldn't tell from where it was coming or where it was leading.

"You seem troubled," announced a voice from behind her.

Eve turned around to see an attractive young woman with long blonde hair that cascaded in soft waves down over her shoulders smiling at her from one of the beach chairs on the deck. She had the most striking blue eyes Eve had ever seen. They were a bright cerulean blue, like an icy glacial lake reflecting the brilliance of a noon sky.

"Yes, I suppose I am." Eve shyly smiled back.

"Hard to leave, isn't it?" She tilted her head slightly, her eyes gazing out over the calm, peaceful water.

Eve walked over, sat down on the only other chair on the deck and stared meditatively out over the lake. The first rays of sunlight were shining up over the horizon, breaking the mist's caress on the water's surface as it rose in feathery wisps.

"Yes," she said resolutely, "it is."

They were both silent for some time as they watched the morning sun crest the sandy dunes, its golden rays caressing the treetops as the mist and water shimmered with their beautiful dance.

"Do you come up here often?" Eve asked, reluctantly taking her eyes away from the view.

The woman smiled at her. "No, this is my first time here. It's absolutely beautiful, isn't it?"

"I've been on several vacations, but this is by far the best one I've ever had. It was a real joy just to be a part of these lovely surroundings." She smiled back. Reaching over the arm of the chair, she extended her hand to the young woman. "My name's Eve, by the way."

"I'm Grace. Pleased to meet you." She smiled and reached across the small void between the chairs, cordially shaking Eve's hand. "You seemed deep in thought. If you don't mind my asking, is something bothering you?"

Eve leaned back into her chair and sighed. "No, I don't mind your asking. But to be honest with you, I'm not exactly sure what's troubling me." She looked over at Grace and shrugged her shoulders in defeat. "I had a wonderful week. Perhaps it's just hard to leave, after all," she answered.

"Hmm. Could be, I suppose, but you don't sound terribly convinced," Grace replied, looking intently at Eve.

Eve laughed. "No, I guess I'm not." She sat in quiet reflection for a moment. *How do I describe a feeling I, myself, don't even understand?* "I'm just down, I guess." She looked across at Grace. "I can't really explain it. I just don't feel … right. I really did have a wonderful vacation. There's just no rational reason for me to feel the way I do."

"Being rational, I suspect, has little to do with it," Grace offered.

Eve smiled politely but quickly dropped back into her silent musing. She felt a deep inner desire to just unload everything, to discharge, to release all her burdens onto this complete stranger. *But wouldn't that be selfish of me?* she wondered, *to encumber this poor woman with all my issues? Besides, how could this woman possibly relate to all the various intricacies in my life? Does she have kids too? Is she married or working?* She doubted it, looking across at Grace. She seemed far too serene to be responsible for children, a husband and a career to boot.

"Are you here by yourself?" Grace interrupted her reverie.

"Oh, no, I'm here with my family. My husband took our two boys out fishing this morning, so I have the day to myself. What about you?"

Grace smiled. "That seems to be a popular hobby around here. My husband got up at a ridiculous hour to take our kids fishing down at the old mill. Perhaps they'll run into each other in their quests for the prize catch of the day."

They sat smiling at their shared coincidences for a moment. But when Eve's eyes travelled back over the water, the veil of melancholy slipped quickly over her features again, and she let the mood pull her back down as she dropped deep into thought. She looked over at Grace and, deciding to throw caution to the wind, she inquired, "Do you ever feel as though you're not completely fulfilled? That there is really nothing major to worry about or complain about and yet … and yet you just don't seem happy?" She struggled to clarify. "I mean, I am happy. I'm happy with my life and my situation but …" She paused. "I just don't know." She tucked a wayward lock of hair behind her ear, searching for elucidation and feeling utterly lost.

"I used to," Grace replied honestly, "but I don't anymore. I found what I was looking for."

"Really?" Eve's interest was piqued. "And what was that?"

Grace smiled. "Why, the same thing that you're searching for, I suppose. I wanted to feel fulfilled and whole, and," she replied, her smile growing wider, "now I do."

"And just how did you manage that?" Eve wondered.

"Well …" Grace stretched languorously. "I started looking in the right places."

Eve was silent for a moment. "Right places, huh? And where exactly did you look?"

"Well, I started looking in here." She tapped her head and her heart. "And I stopped looking out there." She waved her hand, encompassing the water, the sky, the air, everything. "Then eventually, not right away, mind you, but eventually, I figured it out."

"Figured what out?" Eve asked.

"How to be truly happy," Grace replied simply.

Eve considered that. It certainly would be nice to know how to be happy, truly happy. She looked over at Grace, examining her for a moment. She was married and had kids, so she would certainly understand the stress and strain of responsibility and unequivocal love, but ... "Do you mind my asking what you do for a living?"

"Well, I stayed home with my children until I felt they were grown enough to handle my returning to work. I've only been back for a few years now."

"Really?" Eve shook her head in disbelief. "Me too! When we started having children, my husband and I decided that it was best that I stay home with the kids. It's only recently that I've returned to the workforce. I only work part-time in the evenings, but I'm also taking university night courses in an effort to upgrade my degree."

Perhaps that's what's troubling me, she reasoned. *Perhaps I'm just feeling overwhelmed by all my chosen responsibilities and commitments, never mind that hockey and indoor soccer season lurk around the corner menacingly. Maybe I need to slow down and simplify my life.* But no, that didn't fit either. She'd been home for five years and desperately needed to engage in the adult world again, even if that meant late nights at the store and university and early morning car pools to school and hockey practice. She reflected on what Grace had said about looking in the right places and had no concept of which places she was looking in, or whether they were even the right ones. "What did you mean by 'out there' when you spoke about looking for happiness?"

"Well, people tend to look outside themselves for happiness. We strive for material success, like that dream house or the next rung on the corporate ladder. We seek admiration from our peers, or we look desperately to find happiness in the arms of that perfect person. Then, when these don't work or we do not obtain them, we may look for happiness in more destructive ways. Perhaps we turn to substances like alcohol or drugs to blur the edges of our dissatisfaction, or we obsess about sex or food or even shopping." Grace smiled. "Although a little shopping never really hurt anyone." She laughed, winking at Eve. "It's all about moderation."

Eve returned Grace's smile. "I must admit, I never thought shopping was destructive, but after looking at our Visa balance, perhaps Tom, my husband, would disagree," she mused. "But I can't see how success is a negative thing. I mean, don't we all want to be successful? Shouldn't we be striving toward that?"

"Success is fine, in and of itself. In fact, we need a certain amount of it to ensure we have the basic necessities in life, like a roof over our heads and food on our tables. Even a little extra is fine. It's nice to have some luxuries and to be able to play, but we cannot *hinge* our happiness on the achievement of these things. When we finally achieve these desires it may feel good for the moment, but eventually the novelty wears off, leaving us with a hollow feeling that will need to be filled again."

"You know, it's interesting that you would say that. We had been hoping for some time that Tom would get a big promotion. He had worked really hard to meet his sales quota and was at the top of the team, so we figured it was coming. We were really looking forward to a raise to help us out financially," she added. "When he finally got the job, we were really excited to begin with. But the new job involves a lot more travel, and because he has even tighter objectives, he's more stressed now than he ever was before, working even longer hours to try to compensate. I hardly see him anymore." She paused. "You know, this is the first vacation we've taken as a family in ... well, a long time." She looked back over the water. The sun had burned off all the mist, and she felt a warm breeze lift the hair gently from her neck.

"It's very easy to lose ourselves when we're caught up in the ego's never-ending desires. We lose sight of where our happiness truly comes from, and we forget our priorities in a blind desire for success and consumption," Grace reasoned.

"Sometimes I feel lost myself, you know," Eve commented, looking over at Grace. "Not sure about what I want or what will make me happy. I have a small part-time job, which I thoroughly enjoy. It gives me a nice break from the kids, but I just don't feel fulfilled. I wonder if I should go back to school full-time. If I do, I can finish upgrading my skills, which will allow me to contribute more financially. However, it would certainly add a great deal more stress to my life. And," Eve reflected, "as the kids get older, they seem to need me less and less, though I know they'll always need me to some degree. I just can't justify staying at home when they're at school all day." She sighed. "I've put so much on hold in my life ... and I have no clue as to what I want to do with my future."

"Well, part of the problem is your impressions of the future. However, I have to ask why you feel you need to justify your actions. You said you couldn't rationalize staying at home when the kids go back to school. Why not?"

"Why not? Well, because I wouldn't be *doing* anything!" She looked across at Grace, dumbfounded.

"Would your kids be coming home for lunch?"

"Well, yes. I suppose if I wasn't working they would. Otherwise, they would take their lunch. Why?"

"If you stayed home, you could see them off to school, be home for their lunch and be there after school for them. So really, you 'wouldn't be doing anything' for about five hours a day. What is it about those five hours that unsettles you?" Grace questioned.

"Nothing unsettles me about being home. It's just that I could be out earning money or working toward a career instead."

"What if you took a nap or read for the sheer pleasure of it?"

Eve's mouth dropped open and her eyebrow lifted at the scandalous suggestion.

Grace smiled. "Or, if upgrading your skills is so important, could you perhaps take some courses online or figure out a way to earn money from home? Are any of these options a possibility for you?"

"I suppose I could take courses online, but taking naps would definitely be out of the question." Eve laughed and shook her head in disbelief.

"What's wrong with naps? Even Thomas Edison, the great American inventor, felt that naps were essential, never wasted time."

Grace had posed the question so flippantly, Eve had to stop and carefully study her passive expression. She knitted her brows together in consternation. "Even if I could take a nap during the day, why would I?"

"There are some things we do by sheer survival instinct, a deep, inner knowing that keeps us safe from danger, like not touching a hot stove. Other things we feel guided to do by our intuition, like when we decide to finally make that phone call, which results in a new job or new relationship. But most of the things we do, Eve, are because we unconsciously feel compelled or obliged to do them. They have nothing at all to do with instinct or listening to our gut.

"We feel compelled to act a certain way or say certain things because of our belief patterns and habitual ways of responding or thinking about life. You feel you *need* to earn money or work toward a career rather than just taking some time to rest or read for pleasure for *you*. You would feel as though your time was being wasted or used frivolously. Don't you think there are people out there who do just that, who enjoy finding some quiet time during the day all to themselves? Perhaps they just putter around their house or in their garden. Or perhaps they work on some art project or hobby. What makes it okay for them and not you?" She raised her eyebrow, giving Eve a questioning look.

"Perhaps they already have great jobs or are retired and have lots of time on their hands?" Eve quipped.

Grace shook her head. "No, it's all about perception—each person's belief, or view, about any given situation determines their thoughts and actions," she stated simply. "It's your *belief* that taking time for yourself is wasteful and unproductive; and that makes something as innocent as taking a nap unacceptable in your mind.

"For others, their belief *justifies* those actions; it's okay to take naps. I want you to realize that *what you believe* creates your comfort or discomfort and, in the end, your happiness or unhappiness. Take your belief in the future, for example. Your perception, Eve, is somewhat problematic, in that you seem to be living your entire life in the future."

Eve's head was spinning. "What do you mean, I'm living in the future?"

"I mean that you are focusing all your attention on the future. You keep thinking that if you can just change things, everything will be better in a week or in a few years or even tomorrow. What about today? Now? How can you be happy *right now*? You say you don't know what to do with your future. But what are you doing *right now* to make yourself happy?"

Eve wasn't quite sure how to respond to that, but she quickly realized that it was meant as a rhetorical question.

Grace continued. "You are spending too much of your present energy contemplating your future happiness, and very little of you is actually grounded right here in the present moment. Energy flows in and out of us, and we need to appreciate where we are spending it. If we think of energy as a limited commodity, depending upon where we decide to spend it, it either translates into a *good* investment or a *bad* investment.

"So if we make a decision and our action or choice inspires, energizes or revitalizes us, we can consider that a *good* investment of our energy. If, on the other hand, our decision or choice weakens or drains our energy, enthusiasm, inspiration or motivation, then we can consider that a *bad* investment of our energy."

She considered Eve for a moment. "You say you want to find happiness or peace of mind, but your energy is flowing out of you into future events and future dreams. In essence, you have put all your energy, your money, down on that red twenty-one in a game of roulette. What are the odds of getting a windfall on your gamble?"

"Pretty remote, by the sounds of it," Eve conceded sombrely as she looked down at her feet. The water sparkled between the wooden slats of the deck beneath her.

"The only guarantee in life is change. When you are lost in the promises of some distant future, waiting for the magical day when you will finally be happy, all your energy is draining toward some future event, with little left over for enjoying the here and now. You need to spend your energy wisely, Eve, by learning how to accept what is happening in your life right now. By making peace with your present circumstances, you will get a far greater return.

"That's not to say that your life at present is all bliss and flowers," Grace acknowledged, raising her hands as she shrugged. "You are working toward a future goal, which is a noble endeavour, but hoping that these actions will make you happier later is a waste of your energy, and it doesn't help to make you any happier now.

"Accepting the present does not mean you give up any hope of changing your situation, but it does mean that in order to make any real change, you have to first accept where and who you are. Right here, right now!" Shielding her eyes with her hand, Grace pointed toward the dazzling horizon. "We all think that the future out there is full of wondrous possibilities, but everything wonderful happens in the here and now."

Grace reached into her bag, took out two water bottles and passed one to Eve, who accepted it gratefully.

"Thank you," Eve said, looking toward the far end of the deck. The sun's rays on the dark wood created undulating waves of heat that rose upward into the cooler air. "I was just feeling a bit parched. It's like you read my mind."

"I figured since it was warming up nicely, you might like a drink. I know I was getting thirsty."

Twisting off the bottle cap, Grace took a long, measured drink before picking up on the previous conversation. "In order to help you realize that what you are doing in the here and now is affecting your ability to find lasting happiness, you need to get rid of *shoulds* and *shouldn'ts*!"

"Why should I get rid of *shoulds* and *shouldn'ts*?" Eve asked, bewildered.

"Well, you shouldn't do or get rid of anything, but if you want to find the root causes that are holding you back from finding true happiness, you need to consider what saying the words *should* and *shouldn't* means to you. When you say *should* or *shouldn't*, you have to place the word *believe* in front of it. For example, 'I believe I should do this' or 'I believe I shouldn't do that.' But whose belief is it? Is it a belief based on *intuitively knowing* yourself and your innermost dreams and desires, knowing what will make you happy and feel good? Or is it a belief based on the *expectations* that others or we, ourselves, place upon us?"

Eve took a sip of the cool, refreshing liquid. "I'm a little baffled as to why I need to stop using *should* and *shouldn't*. I mean, those words are part of everybody's lexicon. How am I supposed to stop saying them?" she wanted to know. She looked across at Grace expectantly.

Grace put down her water bottle and clarified. "It's easy to stop saying them when you understand what their use implies. By observing your use of *should* and *shouldn't* in the present moment, you begin to catch a glimpse of your unconscious behaviours—which is essential because awareness guides your steps on the path to fulfillment. You need to be aware of your patterns before you can change them. But you also need to examine the use of those fascinating words in context with the past and the future.

"Saying the words *should* or *shouldn't* whenever we contemplate or ruminate on something that has happened in the past is a waste of our precious energy. Essentially, we are creating undue stress for ourselves by worrying about a situation we cannot change. If it happened in the past, we cannot retract or change it. Wishing it were something other than what it really is, by saying 'I should have done this,' or 'I should have said that' just keeps us locked in a cycle of suffering and unhappiness.

"If we project *shoulds* or *shouldn'ts* into the future, we will create an endless supply of grief for ourselves as we question our decisions and choices over and over again. 'Should I say something?' 'Should I do that?' We will never be able to guarantee a safe, perfect outcome no matter how hard we try.

"We have vivid imaginations, and we can create wonderfully catastrophic outcomes just by contemplating whether we *should* or *shouldn't* do something." Grace shook her head in amusement. "Consider sending your children outside at dusk in the summer without bug spray on. If your children come home with mosquito bites, not only will you worry about what the *future* may hold—ranging from mild symptoms of West Nile to full-blown encephalitis and death, but you will then berate yourself about your *past* decision to send them outside without the bug spray on to begin with."

"I see what you mean. But you forgot the part where people accuse me of being a terrible mother and blame me for my child's death, which will

lead to my husband and me divorcing before I'm sent to jail for neglect."
Eve laughed at her exaggeration.

"Wow, you've certainly got quite an imagination, Eve!" Grace chuckled.
"But you can see how we cause needless suffering, stress and worry for
ourselves with our constant questioning and doubts. If we are wondering
whether we *should* go back to school or *should* look for a better job, we are
pursuing those choices in an effort to bring about a different future. This
isn't a bad thing, in and of itself, but in this context we are *expecting* one of
those options to bring us happiness in the future. We are looking *out there*
for our happiness. 'If I make the right choice, if I just do the right thing,
I will finally be happy—tomorrow!' That's quite a gamble!"

She looked over at Eve. "You say you are lost and uncertain about your
life's direction, but your expectations have you living in the future based
on a misguided belief in what you think will make you happy."

"I don't feel I have misguided beliefs," Eve responded, slightly dazed.
"And what do expectations have to do with this?" She shook her head in
an effort to clear the confusion.

"What makes you happy, Eve?"

"What makes me happy?" Eve stopped and stared blankly at Grace for
a moment. It seemed like an easy enough question, yet she had to roll the
words around in her mind. *What makes me happy?* She wondered. "Hmmph!
Well, I suppose I'm happy when everything in my life flows, when my kids
are healthy and happy, when Tom and I are connected, when my job is
going well. Basically, when everything just seems right."

"So your belief is that when everyone and everything around you is
perfect, then you are happy." She looked over at Eve and smiled. "And
how often do you live in this utopia?"

"Well …" Eve was taken aback. "Not as often as I'd like," she realized,
and then, striving for honesty, she added in a resigned tone, "rarely,
actually." Her gaze dropped down.

"Your happiness, or lack thereof, Eve, lies in the fact that you *expect* to
be happy when everything in your life is perfect." Grace paused to allow
the significance of that statement to sink in.

"Eve, you rest your expectations on nothing short of the belief in
perfection. So how on earth can you possibly ever be happy?"

Eve was stunned, struck absolutely speechless. What could she say to
that? The force of those words hit her with such an impact that the tears
began to flow unabated.

Grace's eyes, soft with an expression of reassuring understanding, met hers, and Eve felt comforted by Grace's kindness.

"I know this is hard to hear," Grace continued, "but you need to feel the truth in those words. We so often hide our emotions, wanting to be strong or in control. But you really need to *experience* how you feel. Give yourself permission to feel the emotions that come up. Don't stifle them. Sometimes the truth hurts," she reasoned, "but the truth can also set you free."

Chapter 2

Finding Your True Nature

Grace reached into her pocket, stood and walked toward Eve, handing her a tissue.

Putting on a brave face, Eve smiled tentatively. "Thank you." She blew her nose with a loud honk. "I'm sorry. I don't like to cry, and I tend to hold things in." She shrugged her shoulders. "But what you just said really hit me."

Laying her hand softly on Eve's shoulder, Grace just stood there, offering quiet support, and Eve appreciated the gesture.

Giving her shoulder a gentle reassuring squeeze, Grace sat back down. "I know you want everything to be perfect, Eve," Grace said. "It's wonderful to envision your family healthy and happy, a great job and all the circumstances in your life perfect, but holding on to that image, or concept, as your basis for happiness is not a *good* investment of your energy. You are grasping for some future state, or dream, to bring about your every wish and desire. Essentially, you are trying to control life and make it fit into a nice little box for you—and refusing to be happy until it does.

"For many of us, maybe one or two aspects of our lives can flow well, but never everything, and certainly not all the time." She paused and looked thoughtfully over at Eve.

"Even if we manage to get everything in our lives to line up ideally, like the orbits of the heavenly bodies in the sky, it won't last. Life is about change. Nothing can stay *perfect* forever. The shimmer of the copper dulls, the sparkling silver tarnishes, even the brilliance of a diamond will fade given enough time. The problem is not that things die, decay, or change; it's that we *expect* we can control them rather than just accepting them as they are. It's not necessarily the circumstances in life but rather our thoughts about them that we need to work on!"

Eve sniffed audibly and bleakly smiled in understanding. "I know they change, but shouldn't we *want* things to be perfect? Shouldn't I *want* my children to be happy and healthy? Shouldn't I *want* my job and my life to work out?"

"When you use *should* or *shouldn't*, you're asking me to tell you what to think, to give you permission to think a certain way."

Grace raised her hand for dramatic effect. "Stop right there! I want you to use the SoS alert—Should or Shouldn't alert—whenever you think or say *should* or *shouldn't* from this point on in your life. I want you to make a *full stop* in whatever you are thinking, saying or doing!

"Every time you say *should* or *shouldn't*, it's a wake-up call—a *huge* red-light flashing, alarm-bell ringing, earth-shattering beacon to let you know that you are *not* thinking for yourself. What do *you* think, Eve? Is it a good thing to want everyone to be happy and healthy?"

"Yes?" Eve answered pensively.

Graced smiled. "Sure it is. But if you are always expecting things to be that way, what happens when life throws you a curve ball? What happens to your feelings of peace and contentment then?"

"They disappear?" Eve guessed.

"Exactly! When we *expect* things to work out and they don't, we can become sad, angry, weary, depressed, even disillusioned with life. Wanting to be happy is humanity's greatest desire. However, trying to force life, and therefore all of existence, to bend to our will with constant micromanaging and a tenacious need for control is not realistic. And," she added thoughtfully, "it isn't helpful or healthy, since we are essentially gambling our entire life's happiness on whether or not things work out for us."

Eve regarded Grace curiously. She didn't think she was trying to force life or bend events to her will, but she knew she was terribly disappointed when things didn't work out the way she'd expected. "All right, if I can't *expect* everything to be perfect, how am I supposed to be happy then?"

"What if you viewed your life as it's happening right now from a different perspective? One where nothing is lacking, where nothing else is needed to make you happy? Rather than seeing your life through a sense of lack, as if something were missing, see your life as *perfectly flawed* just the way it is and make peace with that."

"And how would I do that?" Eve asked.

"It's simply a matter of *changing your perspective*, your point of view." Grace was silent for a moment. "Eve." Grace smiled charmingly. "Do you know who you really are or what you really want?"

"Yes. Well, no. What do you mean by that?" She looked over at Grace, who was smiling broadly, like a Cheshire cat who'd just caught a mouse. Eve had the distinct impression that perhaps she was the mouse.

"Hold that thought," Grace said, and she looked at the sun high overhead. "The sun is getting pretty strong." She rummaged through her large beach bag and pulled out a broad-brimmed straw hat, placing it gently on her fair, blonde head. Then she grabbed a pair of big, round sunglasses and put them on. She looked like a movie star, her skin delicately bronzed, a beautiful white spaghetti strap sundress perfectly complementing her petite frame.

Eve looked down at her old cut-off jeans and white tank top, feeling a little self-conscious, and then reached into her bag and pulled out her old scratched sunglasses and a well-loved baseball cap. Wishing she looked as effortlessly beautiful as Grace, she pulled her long, blonde hair up into a ponytail and stuffed it through the hole in the back of her cap.

Grace reached back into her bag and pulled out a thermos and two mugs. "I never know who I'm going to meet, so I always come prepared. Would you like some tea?"

Eve laughed. "I'm beginning to think your bag is bottomless." She shook her head in wonder. "But to answer your question, yes, I would love some tea. Thank you."

"It's green tea with a little maple syrup in it. I admit to having rather a sweet tooth."

Eve laughed. "It sounds wonderful. Another thing we have in common."

Eve tucked her empty water bottle into her bag and accepted the proffered tea graciously. She watched as the steam danced around the rim of the mug, disappearing into the brilliance of the day. She took a tentative sip. It was still hot and felt solidly comforting as its reassuring warmth settled in her stomach.

"Sit back and relax, Eve. I'm going to tell you a story." Grace settled into her own chair, tea mug in hand, and began.

"Once upon a time there were two women. They both had two children and demanding jobs. They were married, and their husbands worked late hours in an effort to get ahead. They had mortgages, credit cards and car loans, soccer practices and car pools.

"One day, as they were getting ready for work, their youngest children crawled out of bed with high fevers and couldn't go to daycare. Their husbands had already left for work, and the women themselves couldn't call in sick, as they both had very important meetings that day.

"The women spent the morning calling various relatives and grandparents to see if anyone could watch their youngest for the day. After they settled the arrangements, they noticed their older children had left their projects on the kitchen table—a project that was worth a large percentage of the science mark. It was due today, with a ten percent cut if it was late. Not wanting their sons to lose marks, they knew they would have to drop the projects off at school before they left for work. At this point they were already running quite late.

"As they were pulling into the school parking lot, their husbands called on their cell phones to let them know that they couldn't take the oldest boys to their playoff soccer games in the evening because their bosses had just scheduled a late-day meeting. This meant, of course, that it was up to the women to get their sons to the game, all the while dragging sick toddlers out of bed to accompany them, not to mention first overcoming the logistics of getting home in time and trying to figure out something fast for dinner. Finally, they each made it to the highway, twenty minutes behind schedule, only to run into a congested, immobile traffic jam. And as they sat in the midst of traffic, one of those women was happy and calm."

Eve raised an incredulous eyebrow sceptically and looked across at Grace. "Calm? How could she possibly be calm?"

"There's a difference between these two women. One sees her life through the ego. The other sees her life through her soul, or her true nature. It's really just a matter of perspective. When our perspective is from the ego's point of view, we are caught up in the external world and spend our lives reacting to it. We live our lives propelled by, and engrossed in, what is happening *out there.*" Grace gestured to the water and sky. "And because of that, we are constantly looking outside ourselves for our source of happiness. Just like you, Eve, when you place your happiness on whether other people or events, outside yourself, are in line with your desires.

"The ego is like a heavy cloak that we wear made up of all our memories and past experiences, which seriously affects our perception of the world. Like filters, those memories and past impressions, which are based on our own unique life experiences, tint the world around us. Because of who we are and what we have gone through, the assumptions we have made and the beliefs we carry, we expect the world to behave and look a certain way. And we are constantly interacting and reacting to the world and our lives through the heavy influence of that cloak. Just as a pair of sunglasses alters the colours of the landscape around us, but once we take the shades off, we see the true colours without the influence of the sunglasses. We need to take the cloak, the sunglasses, off. We need to remove the ego in order to see things as they really are.

"The ego also encompasses our personality, our character traits and our ideas of self-worth and self-esteem. Any time we say *I am* ... 'I am tired, I am sad, I am fun-loving, I am a teacher, a friend, a lover' ... any label at all becomes a mask that we identify ourselves with. It's who we *think* we are. Perhaps, Eve, you may see yourself as a mother, wife, daughter, co-worker or student. Or maybe you would describe yourself as funny, compassionate, helpful, strong, responsible or nurturing.

"However, all of the words you typically use to identity yourself are simply projections of the ego. The labels become the mask you wear every day that hides your soul, the true essence of who you really are. You are none of these things, Eve. You are so much more than your labels, masks, sunglasses and cloaks.

"When we live through the ego, we identify with it—we truly believe that is all we are. But there is so much more to us than that. Take our senses, for example. Everything we see, hear, smell, touch and taste captivates us and keeps us enthralled with the outer world. We are constantly looking outward and relaying messages back to map our outer reality and our place within it. But what happens if we just close our eyes for a moment? Our awareness begins to focus inward. And if we plug our ears too we will find our awareness drawn further inward." She motioned to Eve. "Go ahead, give it a try. Notice how your mind becomes quieter and your attention deeper yet more acute."

Eve complied, shutting out the brilliant morning sun and blocking out the sounds of the world around her. She could feel her breath rise and fall in her body, which she hadn't even noticed before. She also realized how silent her mind was, as if she had crawled into a little cave inside her head, where it was very peaceful and comfortable. She smiled to herself. Such a little thing, closing one's eyes and plugging one's ears, and yet it made such a remarkable difference.

Grace's voice reached Eve from beyond her cave. "Once you open your eyes and unplug your ears ..." She spoke just loudly enough for Eve to hear, so Eve opened her eyes and let her hands fall back to her sides. "Once you open your eyes and ears again, you return to processing your external world and lose touch with that quietness that was happening a mere moment ago. You become identified once more with this *person*, this ego identity, who sees this and hears that, who likes the taste of this or the feel of that. However, if you block your senses, there is a quiet presence right there under the surface, irrespective of what you see with your eyes or hear with your ears."

"I don't understand. How am I identifying with what I hear, see or smell?" Eve wondered.

"What if I said the word *cat*, Eve? What do you see in your mind?" Grace asked.

Eve thought for a moment. "A cute, fuzzy black-and-brown-coloured cat, like the one we had when I was a kid. She was very spirited—she would bite my ankles and meow madly if I didn't feed her soon enough." Eve laughed, fondly remembering the cat.

"And if I said the word *rose*, what do see?" Grace asked.

"I see a beautiful, pale pink rose, with blossoms the size of my hand, that greets me every morning when I look out the window toward my garden while enjoying my cup of tea."

"What does it smell like?"

"It has a sweet, heady fragrance, and whenever I walk past it in the garden, I feel transported, happy, as if I could drift away on its glorious perfume." Eve smiled.

"So you, Eve, are someone who thinks fondly of a cat from her childhood and feels happy when she smells roses. What if I asked someone else those same questions? Would they picture the exact same things as you did, or something different? Would their recollections, experiences, emotions, thoughts or descriptions be different?"

"Yes, of course they would."

"Right! We each have our own impressions and perspectives because we each have unique life experiences.

"There's a good exercise to help you discover what the ego is and how it influences us." She looked over at Eve. "Are you willing to give it a go?"

"The exercise, you mean? Sure, why not?"

"Okay, good. I want you to get comfortable, close your eyes and really think about what I am saying."

Eve put the mug down on the deck beside her and closed her eyes. She felt the warm morning sun on her face, and she smiled. She hadn't had any plans for today when she woke up this morning. She certainly hadn't expected any of this to happen, but she was oddly comforted and grateful that it had. Everything Grace said resonated with her, and she was eager to find out more.

"Ready?" Grace asked.

"Ready!"

"The first thing I'm going to have you do, Eve, is focus on your breath. You can do this part anytime you feel stressed, or overwhelmed; it is a wonderful way to become grounded and centered. All you need is a quiet, comfortable place where you can sit or lie down and not be disturbed.

"Without using words to describe or create commentary on what is happening, follow your inhale and exhale as it moves rhythmically throughout your body. As you breathe, so does every one of the trillions of cells in your body.

"Try to imagine your entire body breathing with you. Visualize your breath as waves. As you inhale, imagine the wave of your breath rolling to the shore, filling you from your toes all the way up to your fingers, all the way up to the crown of your head. Then, as you exhale, feel the wave flowing away from the shore, and as it does, release the breath from the crown of your head through to your fingertips, down to your toes. Breathe with each wave, filling your body with breath on each inhale; release, surrendering your body, on each exhale.

"Be aware of every moment of your breath. From the moment the inhale starts, follow it through to its middle and watch as it flows effortlessly into the exhale. Watch the exhale through its middle, and follow it to its end as it flows softly back into the inhale.

"Take a few minutes to connect with your breath. If thoughts come into your mind, don't worry; just let them pass, bringing your awareness back to the waves of your breath."

Eve watched her breath, feeling her mind become calm as the breath flowed in and out.

"How do you feel?"

"Good." She smiled, her eyes still closed. "The breathing makes me feel calm and peaceful."

"Excellent. Now you are ready to move on. Allow your breath to return to an easy, natural rhythm while I talk you through relaxing your body, one muscle at a time. I want you to take all the time you need, moving slowly, visualizing and feeling each part of your body as you start to relax it.

"Allow your unconscious to take control of your breathing—let your body breathe any way it wants. Let it go wherever it wants.

"I want you to bring your awareness to your toes. Relax your toes. Relax the top of your feet, the bottom of your feet, even the sides of your feet. Let them fall away from your body. Let them move out any way they want. Then take that feeling of relaxation into your legs. Relax your legs from your ankles all the way up to your knees and then all the way up to your hips.

"Completely relax your abdomen; don't hold in your tummy. Just let it all go. Relax the muscles throughout your chest and ribcage, feeling the breath move effortlessly throughout the torso. Relax your entire spine. Feel the lower back release, the middle back release and the upper back release.

"Now take your awareness into your fingers. Relax your fingers, the back of your hands and the palms of your hands. Let go of any gripping or holding in your hands. Feel the relaxation move from your wrists up to your elbows and from your elbows up to your shoulders. Completely relax your shoulders.

"Release any tension in the back of your neck and the sides of your neck. Let your throat soften. Relax your jaw. Soften the muscles around your mouth. Soften the muscles around your eyes. Feel your entire face relax. Release all the muscles throughout your entire scalp.

"I want you to visualize that wave of relaxation moving throughout your whole body. If there is any area that is resisting, just pay extra attention to that part of your body, asking it gently to release and let go."

Eve sighed, her body melting into the chair.

"Now that you look completely relaxed, Eve, I'm going to help you figure out what the ego is by discerning what your soul or your true nature is not. I want you to really try and visualize what I'm about to say. The key is not to rush.

"Keeping your eyes shut, imagine a shelf in front of you. See if you can literally picture a shelf in front of you. If you can't see the shelf, try to at least get a sense of one being right there in front of you, so close that you could reach out and touch it.

"Then, on that shelf, visualize an empty shoebox. Take as much time as you need, to truly *feel* the imagery, to get a sense of the shoebox and the shelf being right there, tangible and real.

"I'm going to have you place all the things that you identify with into that shoebox—all the different parts of the ego that you believe make up who you are.

"Since you are placing everything you falsely identify with into that shoebox, start by placing your five senses into the box. *Feel* a sense of what you would be like if you could see, taste, hear, touch and smell things without any associations—without any understanding, memory or meaning. I want you to picture yourself without any attachment or relationship to words—all words. Remove all the *meaning* behind everything you see, touch, hear, smell and taste and then place all the words or verbal messages, memories and experiences attached to your senses into the box. They are not who you are—you are not your senses. Just see without thinking, smell without discerning, hear without wondering, touch without associating and taste without prejudice. Remove all the ego senses and place them into the shoebox, until there is only the essence, or pure sensation, remaining—void of any thoughts attached to them.

"Take your time, *feel* yourself lifting these senses from your body and mind, placing them into the shoebox. Notice what it feels like once your senses have been lifted from your body and mind. Words like *cat* or *rose* no longer have any relevance—they are *just words,* devoid of any past, present or future associations.

"Now I want you to place all your emotions into that shoebox. There is so much more to you than just your emotions. All of your fear, your guilt, your anger, your doubt, your sadness—any negative emotions that you are feeling—place them all into the box because *you* are not your emotions. For a moment, try to just visualize all the negative emotions you've ever felt. Visualize taking these emotions and placing them all into the shoebox, so that there are no longer any negative emotions left in your body or mind whatsoever. Imagine yourself completely free of all negative emotion. Take all the time you need.

"Now, take all your past memories and place them into the shoebox. Memories can be painful, and they can also be filled with joy, but memories are not who you are. You don't need them to exist. So, for a moment, just put them all into the box. Visualize all the feelings and images connected to the past, with all their associated emotions and messages, and place them all into the box. I want you to feel your heart and mind lighten as you place your past into the shoebox.

"Also, place your beliefs and biases—all your ideas about how things should or shouldn't be or how people, yourself included, should or shouldn't be—into the shoebox. Take any resistance to change and place it into the box.

"Take your personality, all the adjectives and descriptors you use to describe yourself, and place them all into the shoebox. You are not your personality. You are much more than that, so for now just place them all into the shoebox. Whenever you say you are funny, smart, a hard-worker, etc., you are describing yourself. Place all those descriptive words and the feelings they evoke in you into the box. Lift out from your body and mind all of your associations about *who you are* and place them into the shoebox.

"Now, add the many masks you wear on a daily basis. These are the labels that you use to identify yourself—the concepts that you are a mother, a friend, a sister, a daughter, a teacher, a worker, a healer, a victim—any label you use to define who you think you are. Place them all into the shoebox. Really search your mind for all your labels; remove them from *who you are* by placing them all into the shoebox. Again, take your time and really feel yourself removing these labels from your body and mind.

"Now that you have taken all your emotions, your senses, your past experiences and memories, your beliefs and biases, your personality and labels, removed them from your body and mind, and placed them into the shoebox, you will have a sense of being without all that *other stuff* that occupies the same headspace. All that *other stuff*, those associations and feelings, are all over there on the shelf, in the shoebox—completely separate from you right now.

"You are still here, calm and peaceful, yet all that *other stuff* is over there in the shoebox. You can see it, but it is completely separate from you right now. So if you are not all those things, then who are you? Really connect with that concept. If you are not all those things—because they are all over there in that box—then who are you?"

Grace was silent for a moment. "You may be drawing a complete blank, unable to define yourself. Welcome to your soul!"

When Eve opened her eyes, Grace continued. "You have just discovered the true essence, the *aliveness*, the intrinsic *being-ness* of who you are—and that true essence is found in every living thing on this planet and beyond. It is separate from your sensations, memories, thoughts and emotions.

"We can capture a glimpse of our soul, or true essence, when our mind is quiet, when we are absorbed in something that we are passionate about, when we commune in stillness with nature, enjoying a beautiful sunset or puttering in our garden. When we are pursuing a sport or hobby, such as dancing, or when we are creating art, we find moments when time seems to stand still and we are acutely conscious of our *being-ness*—we are still aware of our surroundings but are enveloped in a sense of peace and contentment."

Eve nodded. "You know, years ago I used to get that sensation, a feeling of timelessness when I was painting. I can still find it sometimes when I'm gardening."

"The tranquility, calmness and peace you felt while painting or gardening, Eve, is a beautiful example of a moment when you experienced your true essence—who you really are. That tranquility is ultimately *you*, experiencing yourself and your life through your soul—and your soul is limitless and full of unbridled potential.

"On the other hand, the ego, which fits quite nicely in that little shoebox of yours on the shelf, keeps you caught up in the world of reactions and associations. It creates a chasm in your awareness, and you become separated from your soul, your true essence.

"The ego has a great deal invested in its opinion of itself and keeps our minds constantly jumping from one external desire to the next in order to maintain that separation. After all, if we are always looking outward, we won't discover our soul, nor will we even know where to look for it, and that is exactly what the ego wants. It has a real palpable energy of its own, and to realize that we have a choice in how we see the world is a real threat to the ego's existence. It will do everything in its power to keep us locked in the struggle caused by this separation, by pulling us toward the next external thing to make us happy. Happiness can only be achieved by finding peace within, not by looking outside ourselves for our contentment. Happiness lies in the centre of our being, our very soul, and when we are separated from that centre, we are unhappy. We search throughout our entire lives trying to find the next fix to see if that will finally make us happy. We might find happiness for a moment, but it never lasts. It can't." Grace pointed to her heart. "True happiness and peace can only be found deep inside, in the centre of our being."

Grace looked across at Eve. "So, to return to our story about the two women stuck in traffic. There you are, Eve, full of pain, separation, anxiety and frustration, bound by the pull of the ego—unlike the other woman who has found her centre and no longer lives her life caught up in the roller-coaster ride, being thrown from one moment to the next."

"Okay. Let me see if I have this straight." Eve was quiet for a moment. "You're telling me that I am unhappy because I am living through the ego, which I will recognize because I can define it with labels or adjectives? So if I say something like, 'I am *angry*,' or 'I am a *friend*,' then I am caught up in the ego. But if I can't describe or label who I am, then I am living through my soul?" Eve shook her head trying to make sense of the concept, as if she were trying to solve a giant jigsaw puzzle. "I must admit, you have thrown out some pretty esoteric stuff here."

Grace laughed. "Well, something like that, yes. But what I really want you to take away from all this is the *feeling* or *sense* that you could exist without all that *other stuff*. That when everything was placed into that shoebox, therefore quite separate from who you are, you were able to have an authentic experience of yourself just as you are."

"Yes, I got that," Eve said, smiling keenly. "Actually, it was really neat because when you said, 'You may be drawing a blank,' I really was. Once I took away my emotions, my labels and all that other stuff, I had no idea what to call what was left. But yes, interestingly enough, I was definitely aware that I was still there, despite getting rid of everything else."

"Good. You had a direct experience of your soul—that space within your awareness that exists separately from the ego. It's always there. It always has been and always will be. You've just forgotten how to find it."

"Okay." Eve was game. "If I've found it, what am I supposed to do with it?"

"Learn how to stay there."

Eve stared blankly across at Grace. "Learn how to stay there? Grace, you do realize that you speak in tongues? I feel like I'm going around in circles!"

Grace chuckled. "Remember the story about the two women in the car?

"Yes," Eve replied. "I do."

"The events they both experienced while trying to get to work that morning might be labelled as chaotic …"

"That's an understatement," Eve interjected.

Grace laughed. "Well, they didn't faze one of the women—she was able to remain calm, cool and collected throughout the entire ordeal."

Eve looked over at Grace and eyed her critically. "I don't see how she could have been so calm, given everything she had thrown at her. I can't even imagine how someone could be calm in that situation!"

"Well," Grace explained, "learning to live through your soul or true essence helps you stay centered and grounded when your world turns upside down and it feels as though everything is out of your control.

"The calm woman wasn't expecting anything in particular to happen, so she could deal with whatever was happening with better efficiency and less anxiety—she experienced the morning through her soul.

"The other woman, *expecting* a smooth morning getting off to work, experienced the morning through her ego and, as such, was bombarded with obstacle after obstacle. She was pulled along from one event to the next, and everything was out of her control. Her toddler getting sick was out of her control; her husband being unable to get home early from work was beyond her control. She was pulled down by the undertow of external events and felt like she was drowning, desperately trying to keep her head above water.

"The woman who remained calm throughout was clearly unaffected by the pitches and heaves that buffeted her from every side. By not having any expectations, she was able to stay detached, calm and grounded—none of the morning's events elicited a reaction.

"Here's an analogy of a carriage wheel that might help. You know those old-fashioned wheels that they used for horse-drawn carriages?" she asked Eve. "They had an outer rim attached to spokes that led to the hub, or centre, of the wheel, where the axle was attached."

"Sure, those big wooden wagon wheels, like in the old cowboy movies." Eve smiled.

"Exactly! When you are living through the ego, you are living on the edge of the wheel, on the rim, subjected to all of life's ups and downs. When things are going great, everything is wonderful and you are on top of the world—on the top of the wheel. But when life gets difficult, you are thrust down to the bottom of the wheel, with the weight of the world and your circumstances weighing heavily on your shoulders. You have no control over life's ups and downs; you are driven at the mercy of the ever-changing cycles of consequence. Sometimes you are up; sometimes you are down. Sometimes you are happy; sometimes you are unhappy. This is the realm of the ego.

"Your soul, on the other hand, resides in the hub of the wheel. You are still aware of what is happening in your life. You watch the ups and downs, but you are no longer affected by those fluctuations. You are no longer subjected to the emotional roller coaster of being on the top one minute and then on the bottom the next. You are living your experience from a very different perspective. The centre, or hub, of the wheel is a calm, contented and peaceful place to be. This is the realm of your soul."

Chapter 3

Resurrection through the Past

It was almost noon. The beach was beginning to fill with families eager to take advantage of the glorious weather. Eve stood up slowly, stretching her arms up toward the sky and yawned. "I think my leg has fallen asleep from sitting so long." She looked down, shaking out the pins and needles. "Maybe we could go for a walk along the beach. We have been sitting here an awfully long time."

Graced leaned back in her chair and stretched. "That sounds like a wonderful idea."

Feeling the blazing sun beat down on her shoulders, Eve reached into her bag and pulled out her sunscreen. Applying it liberally to her slightly bronzed skin, she offered the bottle to Grace. "Would you like some sunscreen?"

"Yes, thank you," Grace replied, and smoothed the lotion onto her skin.

Eve waited for Grace to finish. Placing the bottle back into her bag, she hopped down onto the sand. Grace followed.

The beach stretched for miles in either direction, offering a luxuriously soft landscape under Eve's bare feet. She had a pair of sandals packed in her beach bag, but she loved the feel of the velvety sand between her toes. Her kinks worked themselves out nicely, and she looked across at Grace, who had fallen into step beside her. "Thanks for agreeing to walk with me. I almost didn't want to interrupt our conversation for fear you might have to leave, but my leg was going to explode if I didn't get up and shake it out."

Grace smiled. "I think stretching our legs was a great idea, and as for leaving—there's no place I'd rather be."

They walked to the edge of the sand where the glistening water lapped gently at the shore. Strolling along the cool, squelching surface, Eve left transient footprints in the sand; each wave wiped out all traces of her journey. Eve thought about the wagon wheel and the two women in the car. *Wouldn't it be incredible to actually be able to sit through stressful situations and not be affected by them?* she marvelled. It seemed impossible, like something out of a science fiction movie.

Shaking her head, she turned to Grace. "Remember the story you told about the women in the car?"

"Yes," Grace replied, nodding in affirmation.

"Well, I'm having a hard time accepting the idea that after dealing with all that chaos, *anyone* could sit in that car, calm and peaceful. While I don't profess to have the most stressful life, I know my stress level is usually hovering on *don't push me,* and even the slightest little thing can often set me off. I think if I were in that car, stuck in traffic, after having that kind of morning, I would be seriously stressed out!"

"Stress is a very interesting phenomenon," Grace said. "Not only does it seriously affect our health, physiologically and psychologically, but it robs us of our capacity to handle situations and stimuli. When we are living through the ego, we have a powerful stress threshold, or breaking point. We can only handle so much. Then along comes that final straw that pierces through our armour, and we lose our reasoning, our objectivity and our minds. Sometimes, it's a cumulative effect, like the multitude of circumstances that affected the women in the car, but other times specific people or certain situations immediately trigger us into oblivion."

Eve interjected, "Oh, I know that one all too well! My parents are probably one of my biggest triggers. It doesn't seem to matter how well my day is going; once they start in on me, I lose it."

Grace smiled. "Parents are really good scapegoats to blame for all our stress and problems, but in reality it is just you and your thoughts that are causing all the strife, not them."

"At this point, I have to disagree with you, Grace. Nothing personal, but for years I've had to listen to my parents' constant barrage about the choices I've made in life. I'm not making up the stress that places on me, and their behaviour is a major cause of the strife in our relationship and subsequently in how I define who I am and what I do."

"How does what they say define who you are or what you do?" Grace asked.

Eve reflected in silence for a moment. "They wanted me to become a teacher," she explained, looking at Grace. "When I went to university, they paid for my tuition. After I obtained my degree, I never went on to become a teacher. It nearly killed me to tell them my decision. I spent many sleepless nights ruminating about it. It was the hardest thing I've had to do."

Eve looked down at her feet, her toes sinking into the cool sand as a rolling wave washed over her ankles. "You see, I'd met Tom during university and fell madly in love with him." She smiled sheepishly. "And it seemed natural to want to get married and start a family. I don't regret my decision. I have two beautiful children, but now that they're getting older and finances are becoming tighter, I've naturally looked at what I should do as far as a career goes. My parents felt that I married too young and that I threw away my career opportunities to settle down too quickly. Don't get me wrong. They are ecstatic about their grandchildren, but they use that argument to support their constant attack on me to go back to school and upgrade my skills. It doesn't help, of course, that they constantly throw guilt at me. They remind me incessantly that they incurred real financial hardship by paying for all of my schooling to ensure that I received a proper education, and I have effectively done nothing with it." She sighed. "I know I should go back to school to become a teacher, but my heart just isn't in it."

"Let me ask you a question, Eve. What motivates you? What compels you to act a certain way or do certain things?"

"I'm not sure I understand the question."

"Well, most of our actions or decisions are based on patterns of behaviour and thought processes that we have learned from our past interactions with our *tribes*. These tribes are our families, our parental or birth family plus any expanded family that now includes a spouse and children. Our tribes also include our relatives and extended families, our community or social networks, our friends and colleagues, our work or school environments, political affiliations, religious communities, ethnic and cultural backgrounds, as well as the entire global framework and network. From the moment we were conceived, these tribes formed our first relationships. Within the context of those relationships, we have learned all our attitudes, our belief systems and the habits or behaviours that we continue to rely on when we interact with life, with its myriad of colourful people and situations. That influence defines how we view others, but just as importantly, it defines how we view ourselves and, specifically, how we view our place and our status in each of these relationships. That is a *lot* of influence!

"At some point in our lives, though, we need to understand that these beliefs that were created so long ago, when the tribe spoke for us and through us, may not be what we need *now*. When you grow older, those favourite shoes no longer fit right; similarly, some of the old beliefs, ideas, prejudices, habits and behaviours may no longer *feel* right to us anymore, may no longer *fit* our lives anymore.

"The reason I asked, Eve, is because I want you to examine what your motivations are. We are going to start by really working on those *shoulds* and *shouldn'ts* of yours!"

"Okay, I'm game. So what is it that's supposed to be motivating me?"

"Well, put simply, *you* are supposed to be the driving force behind what compels or motivates you into action, but for the majority of instances and people, that is rarely the case.

"We are all very good at allowing someone else's opinions to influence and determine what we think and do. We *feel* we *should* act a certain way, and this will always imply that there is a deep expectation from our tribal roots, pulling us back into a familiar way of reacting to life. It is a knee-jerk, unconscious reaction because we *feel*, based on past influence, that we are *supposed* to behave a certain way—to fit in, to be worthy, to be appreciated, to be loved, to be successful, to be accepted." Grace's beautiful blue eyes softened as she smiled. "When we act from this perspective, from these *beliefs*, we are acting out of fear—fear of failure, fear of abandonment, fear of rejection.

"If we learned early in life to respect our elders and were corrected any time we questioned something a person of authority said, can you project how that same belief now, as adults, might affect how we take negative criticism from a boss, parent, co-worker, etc.? Perhaps we would be unable to say anything back, except in our heads, where our thoughts continuously recycle our anger and resentment. Perhaps that *belief* doesn't fit us anymore."

Eve frowned. "My parents always told me not to talk back to my elders, that it was disrespectful. I never considered that it still influences my behaviour now that I'm older."

"Have you ever seen *The Runaway Bride* with Richard Gere and Julia Roberts?"

"Yes, it's a funny movie," Eve said.

"Do you recall how Richard Gere's character asked Julia's if she knew how she liked her eggs? In the movie, every time she got involved with another man, she would cook eggs the way her new lover liked them and then profess that she, herself, preferred her eggs that way too. Since her opinion was influenced by the likes and dislikes of each lover, she took those influences upon herself as a means to define who she was. Thus, with each new relationship, she liked their way of eating eggs the best. When she was confronted with the question of how she liked her eggs, removed from everyone else, she had no clue.

"So many of us have no idea how we like our eggs! We allow everyone else's opinions and beliefs, ideals and perspectives to influence what needs to be uniquely ours to choose—how we like our eggs or careers or life pursuits, our choice of lovers or friends, our interests, clothing, style, etc. In the end, Julia's character figured it out and was a much more balanced, whole person because she defined her likes based on what was intrinsically hers, removed from the biases of others." Grace paused. "It doesn't matter what your parents' perspective is, Eve, nor does it matter what their beliefs or opinions are. What *does* matter is what *you* think—what are *your* ideals, *your* beliefs? What do *you* want to do with your life, Eve?"

Eve looked imploringly at Grace. "I don't know."

"Well, what if we remove your parents from the scenario, just for a moment, so that your parents no longer have any influence over your decisions? What if I could wave a magic wand and resolve the past? Make all your guilt, fears and concerns disappear? I'm going to give you a completely clean slate to start all over, to do whatever it is you'd like to do, right here, right now. No strings attached, just complete freedom to be who you want to be and do what you want to do. For a moment, suspend all disbelief and tell me how you really like your eggs, Eve. What is it that you really want to do?"

Looking out over the water toward the shimmering horizon, Eve stopped walking and sighed. She felt as if she had been thrown into a vacuum and all the air had been sucked out of her. She knew what she wanted to do, but what she wanted to do made no sense and didn't fit in at all with her current life directions or decisions. It was fantasy, not based on real, financial considerations. What she really wanted to do was to create. She wanted to be an artist, but it was only a dream. It wasn't based on reality. Yet, if she was asked, as Grace had just done, there was no question as to what she really wanted to do. She drew a deep line in the wet sand with her big toe, watching the sand part, only to fold back in upon itself, leaving a slight furrow.

"You know," Eve said, staring down at her feet, resuming their walk, "I remember as a kid loving to draw and colour on anything I could find. I found that I looked at things very differently from others—that even the smallest things would catch my attention. A ladybug would captivate me. I would note its colour, the number of dots on its back and then I'd draw it. Everything around me was an opportunity waiting to find expression. When I looked at things, I saw through their mere appearances and felt I could catch a glimpse of their very essence. I tried to convey that essence in everything I drew or painted or sculpted." She looked up, her gaze wandering absently to the golden dunes in the distance. "But I never kept it up. I never continued my art. There didn't seem to be a place in my life that fit its existence or expression. I mean, I draw occasionally for my kids. I remember when Tom took forever to put a new backsplash in the kitchen. I got sick and tired of staring at a blank wall, so I decided to spruce it up by drawing cartoon characters of my kids using permanent black marker on the drywall. I had completely forgotten about it until we remodelled the kitchen this spring. A huge grin washed across my face when we rediscovered them. It used to be such a big part of who I was, and I feel I've lost that. It's like I've lost my passion, and I don't know how to get it back." She looked longingly at Grace. "You know, my kids love stories, and I've taken to writing and illustrating some books that we read at bedtime. I found I was beginning to enjoy it." She shrugged her shoulders. "But it doesn't really matter. There's no magic wand anyway."

"Of course there's a magic wand!" Grace assured her.

Eve looked disapprovingly at Grace. "How can you possibly say that? You can't just change your life like … like that," she protested, snapping her fingers in illustration. "You can't just make all the hurt and guilt and fear suddenly up and disappear. Life doesn't work like that!" She shook her head in disbelief and looked back out over the water. The waves were rolling lazily into and away from the shore in a soft, carefree rhythm. But, in contrast, she felt agitated and slightly impatient at Grace's insistence there was a *magic wand* that can make everything better.

For some time they walked the beach in silence. Restless, unable to determine what to do with this bothersome and bizarre concept, Eve pushed it firmly from her mind. Tilting her head upward, she gazed into the cloudless blue sky. The sun's rays were intensifying. She felt the heat caressing her bare arms and neck as they walked. It was going to be a very warm afternoon.

A loud gurgle interrupted the decorous silence. Eve's stomach registered its discomfort as they passed a small café with tables overlooking the beach. Eve's face flushed with crimson embarrassment, and they both laughed.

Grace looked over at the café and back at Eve and smiled. "Perhaps we could have some lunch?"

"Yes, I think that's a lovely idea. My treat." She smiled at Grace as they made their way through the sand up to the small, intimate patio.

"That's very kind of you. Thank you," Grace said.

They chose a table with a bright red umbrella that overlooked the water. A handsome young waiter, tanned a deep golden brown, flashed them a brilliant white smile as he handed them their menus. Tall, with sandy brown hair, the edges bleached blond from the sun, he looked like a California surfer. Smiling, Eve watched as he sauntered toward the bar. Then she turned her attention to the lunch menu, scanning the offerings.

When the waiter returned, Grace ordered a veggie burger with a garden salad, while Eve chose a chicken Caesar wrap. They split a plate of sweet potato fries between them.

As they ate their lunches companionably, Eve spoke about her past, about growing up in a typical middle-class family, and all that had led her to this point in her life. Grace regaled Eve with some of her adventures, recalling how she searched for meaning in her life and balanced that search while maintaining a family and career. Eve was fascinated at the ease with which Grace seemed to take everything, as if all the trials and tribulations in her life were nothing more than mere changes in the direction of a breeze.

"I can't believe how hungry I was!" Grace said, interrupting Eve's thoughts as she devoured the last morsel on her plate.

Eve laughed. "Yes, me too!" she said, looking in consternation at her own empty plate. "Do you have any room for some dessert?"

"Of course." Grace winked. "There's always room for dessert."

The dessert—a decadent piece of chocolate cake sitting on a plate drizzled with fresh raspberry coulis and accompanied by two forks— arrived. Eve watched in amusement as Grace smiled in abandoned repletion as she savoured each blissful bite. *What is it about this woman?* Eve wondered. They seemed to have so much in common, yet everything about her radiated peace and serenity and an almost childlike joy. Eve felt her spirit lift just from being in Grace's presence and said as much.

Grace smiled. "Do you see that little girl over there on the beach?"

Eve looked over in the direction of Grace's gaze and chuckled. "You mean the one with juice dribbling down her chin?" The little girl in question couldn't have been more than three years old and was happily devouring a ripe, juicy peach, completely unconcerned about the sand stuck to her bare arms and legs where the peach juice had created rivulets along her skin.

Grace's entire face lit up when she smiled. She picked up another forkful of chocolate cake. "We are all meant to be able to feel like that, to experience the bliss in each moment, no matter how mundane or common. When we are lost in our internal dramas, we miss the beauty in life, we miss the joy in our experiences, and we miss the *gift* in the present. It's in those moments of complete joy and abandon when our soul, our true essence, is literally shining through us. In those moments, we are living life through the *eyes of our soul*, so to speak. The rest of the time we are functioning through the ego.

"When we are enjoying one of those *present* moments, we are *super* conscious, or *super* aware, of our surroundings and our immediate experience. It's like we are actually *living*, not just going through the motions. We are observing or taking in all that is around us and all that is happening to us at that very moment. And in those moments, the pernicious, mental barrage that is our constant companion ceases, and we are just *being*. For a moment, the ego takes a back seat, and our soul shines in the forefront of our consciousness.

"That delightful little girl isn't thinking about what she will do next. She isn't wondering whether she *should* go for a swim or perhaps build a sand castle. She isn't concerned with whether or not she *should* have grabbed a napkin first or whether she *shouldn't* have played in the sand while eating her peach. She is simply lost in the pure pleasure, the enjoyment, of eating her treat, right now. In order to be *in the moment*, we have to stop the mental thought processes long enough to simply enjoy each experience without the running commentary on what's next or what's already happened."

"That seems impossible to me," Eve remarked. "Stopping the commentary, that is. I know I've been able to do that for a *few* moments. Sometimes, while gardening, I've felt that stillness—when I just lose myself in the moment and my mind is completely absorbed in what I'm doing right then and there. Other times while gardening, my mind is anywhere but in the backyard with me," Eve recollected.

"Well, you didn't start out thinking constantly," Grace suggested. "At one point in time you were no different than that little girl—completely absorbed in the moment, in the *now*. The thinking started slowly interrupting your revelry, one thought at a time. Years later, you and everyone else on this planet had developed a very bad habit—the habit of thinking constantly! We were never meant to lose ourselves in our thoughts. That's how we lose contact with our inner voice, our soul or true essence. Our soul is always trying to get our attention, to help us remember what it was like to just *be*—to be peaceful and fulfilled. Unfortunately, with all the racket that our mental cacophony makes, we can't hear it."

The waiter interrupted their conversation. "Would you ladies like anything else, some coffee or tea perhaps?"

Grace looked up. "I would love a decaf coffee, please," she said.

"Make that two," Eve added, smiling into the waiter's bright hazel eyes.

Within moments the waiter returned, setting two steaming mugs of coffee down on the table in front of them. Eve inhaled the deep, rich aroma as she measured out equal amounts of cream and sugar.

Picking up the conversation where they left off, Eve frowned as she stirred the contents of her mug. "And just how, exactly, did we develop this bad habit of thinking constantly?"

"Imagine that you found yourself living beside a major highway, with six to eight lanes carrying cars and transport trucks twenty-four hours a day, seven days a week," Grace said and took a sip of her coffee. "Initially, the din would bother you, even with the doors and windows shut. Eventually, you'd get accustomed to the white noise in the background and wouldn't pay it a second's notice. As the weather turned pleasant, you'd head out into the backyard. At first, you would feel annoyed with the constant clamour as you tried to relax. Eventually, though, you'd be able to have barbeques and parties, completely oblivious to the monotonous sounds of the traffic. It would become a part of your life, and you would resign yourself to living with it. At that point, it no longer poses an issue. You no longer give it even a passing thought.

"But one beautiful summer morning, as you are sipping your tea on the back porch, a far-away accident shuts down the entire highway in both directions. A bee buzzes near your ear, and you flinch as it flies by. A robin chirps happily in the grass as it searches diligently for a juicy worm or grub. A squirrel scampers across the fence, making little scratching noises as it passes along the wood. You smile at the vignette unfolding before your eyes, but then something in your mind registers all this as odd. You look around, trying to discern the cause of your strange sensation. Then it hits you. Silence! The cars have stopped! You stand up to look out over the fence, only to see that the entire highway is empty. You drift, wondering what happened and if it was a really bad accident, which it must have been to close down the entire highway. But then you hear a woodpecker in the little wood lot that runs beside your home. Stopping to listen, you are amazed at all the sounds you can hear. The fountain in your small birdbath creates a lovely trickling sound. You can hear a bevy of buzzing activity over by your flower garden, as well as the calls of distant birds throughout your neighbourhood. In short, you soak in the *silence*. You abandon yourself in the moment, feeling entirely peaceful, serene and happy."

Eve sighed. Listening to Grace describe the transformation, she could actually feel the tranquility suspended in that rare gift of silence.

"Suddenly, you hear a car whiz by, followed by another and another. You stand back up to look over the fence again as the multitude of vehicles come careening back with their exhaust and noise, once again polluting the air around you. You try to listen again for the woodpecker, but it's gone. Heading back inside, you grab your tea, feeling slightly bereft at the loss of the peaceful silence but resigned, once again, to living with the noise. In a few minutes, as you start worrying about the rest of your responsibilities and the day's to-do lists, the stillness of that morning, that magical moment, is completely gone."

"Wow, that's kind of sad. I mean, I can actually feel the loss just hearing you speak about it," confessed Eve quietly.

"That's exactly what happens to us, though. Our thoughts become so constant that they are like white noise. We just plod along through our lives, our monotonous monkey mind chirping and shrieking all day long. Instead of trying to stop it, we just cope with it, as if it's just supposed to be this way, and that's that.

"I know this may upset some people to hear, but Heaven is not up there." Grace pointed to the sky and smiled. "It's in those brilliant, beautiful moments when our mind stills. The idea is to make those moments last until we are living Heaven on Earth. When we experience that bliss, it is a loss to have our mental chatter take it away from us. The good news is, once our soul has had a taste of that experience, it will go out of its way to experience it again, drawing us to find that quiet centre. Our soul is compelled to experience joy, and it will naturally be drawn to things that make us feel joyful."

"Do you mean like the joy I feel when I'm painting or gardening?" Eve asked.

"Yes, absolutely. For others it could be dancing, working out or playing with their children. Anything at all that allows us to feel joy in our lives is an expression of our soul shining forth.

"The point is to find more time to enjoy those activities that offer us the best chance for peace and joy. Unfortunately, we needlessly fill too much of our time with superfluous actions that make us *seem* busy. Think quality, not quantity, here. We will actually keep ourselves constantly doing something or going somewhere, just to avoid slowing down. Now, there's a good, defensive reason for this. If we are not in touch with our soul, or true essence, if we are not living life in the centre of that wheel, then whenever we actually do slow down, our mind is filled with negativity, worry or just plain exhausting mental noise. Who wants to be in communion with that?"

"Not me," Eve acknowledged, shaking her head.

"No one does, but most people don't know they have a choice. They just fill in the gaps so that they don't have to slow down long enough to listen, pushing themselves too hard in their jobs, in their spare time—in their lives." Grace took another sip of coffee. "We create mountains of stress just to avoid ourselves. This is one of the biggest illusions that the ego can play on us. It keeps us looking out there for our peace of mind and tricks us by making us feel compelled to keep looking—harder, longer. When we do engage in the ego's aimless games, there is no way we can hear the gentle yearnings of our soul.

"We have to learn how to be alone with ourselves and sit quietly, without anyone else around to talk to, without so much as a book, without any music, without something to do or some place to go … we have to learn how to just sit and be." Grace looked across and laughed as Eve's mouth dropped in an expression of horror. "Pretty scary stuff," Grace conceded

Eve shook her head. "I can't fathom how to do that. I know that I fill every little crack in my day up with details. I must admit, it never occurred to me that I'm running away from myself, but I do know that when I am just sitting there, doing nothing, I feel compelled to get up and, well, do anything but keep sitting there doing nothing." She laughed. "I am pretty busy with my part-time job, night school courses and looking after the kids, but I also know there are a lot of moments during the day that I fill with really needless stuff, just to keep busy. I could probably stand to lose some of the things that aren't really necessary, like checking out my Facebook page a couple times a day …but then what would I do?"

"That's the problem. Too many people feel that they have to *do* something! You said that just sitting around or taking a nap is out of the question. I asked you then to consider your motives; why you feel you can't stop or slow down. One of the ego's many tactics is to fool us into believing that if we slow down or seem to have nothing to do, then we aren't a value to society, our family or ourselves. Another of the ego's fanciful illusions is our unique *ego identity*, our false—but undeniably *real* to us—identity. If we have convinced ourselves that we are hard-working, superhumans who do not slow down, who push ourselves to our limits … then we have invested a lot of energy and time in that perception, in that persona. The ego wouldn't appreciate it if, all of a sudden, we decided that we didn't want to be superhuman anymore but rather wanted to be just human and even stop to smell the roses now and again.

"'You can't do that!' the ego stresses. 'You have to stay busy. Look, you don't have that high-power job yet. You don't have the American Dream yet, or that shiny new car, or the respect of your mother or father, or the envy of the neighbourhood. Keep working! Keep striving!' the ego demands. And we listen—again and again, we listen. It's very similar to being brainwashed.

"The ego conditions us to act a certain way, behave a certain way, until we are no longer thinking for ourselves, we are just acting. Do you really want to be a projection of everyone else's ideals and beliefs? An actor, who just plays her expected roles or reenacts her unconscious behaviours and habitual patterns over and over again? Or do you want to start living an authentic life where you are the author of your own experience? When *you* decide that you want to *live* your life, rather than just project the ego's desires, you need to learn how to be alone with your definition of 'me, myself and I' and try to find the authentic, the *real* you who is sitting there quietly in the background, just waiting to be discovered."

"Well, how would I do that?" Eve asked.

"You've already experienced your soul in that little exercise we did earlier this morning, the point of which was to get you to quiet your mind. After completely relaxing, you focused on emptying the extraneous details from the false ego identity. You were left with nothing but silence and being. You were completely in the moment. In essence, you were meditating. You were relaxed and focusing on something so completely that your mind became quiet and still. If there were any gift I could give you, Eve, it would be the gift of meditation, or entering the stillness, if you prefer.

"Words are just labels that, in themselves, have no meaning. The associations we place on them create their meaning. Subsequently, if you feel resistance to the word *meditation*, perhaps you can look at it another way—as just entering the stillness and quietude of your own mind. And I promise I'll teach you how to do that. But for now," she said as she watched the waiter put the bill on the table, "we need to get back to our walk. There's something I want to show you."

As they stepped back onto the warm sand, Eve kept a wary eye on Grace, half expecting her to continue the conversation at any moment, but Grace seemed much too intent on her purpose to be wondering about the ramifications of everything they had spoken about. Eve, however, had no such purpose. In fact, she couldn't keep her mind from racing and ruminating on their last exchange. In her swirling mind, she wasn't sure what to grab hold of first. She considered whether she could actually meditate. How was she supposed to keep her mind quiet for any length of time? Eve had no idea, more than convinced that she must have a freeway running along her neural pathways at all times.

Reflecting back on the day's many conversations, Eve was drawn back to Grace's surprising insistence that life could be turned around or changed at the drop of a hat, or with a "magic wand," as she put it. Eve had been to a few counsellors in her day, trying to understand her *issues*, and had occasionally suffered from depression when she felt like life was unfair or when she couldn't seem to get herself out of a funk or rut. But there was certainly no magic wand, no hocus-pocus, that could just make it go *poof!*, that could make the dark clouds disappear when they settled in for their periodic stays. Eve knew she wasn't psychotic; she had problems like everyone else, and she wasn't afraid to talk to someone if she felt she couldn't handle or solve them on her own. She never understood why some people were apprehensive about going to speak with someone. *Sometimes, it's just what the doctor ordered.* She smiled at her own humour.

As she looked around the crowded beach, it seemed as though everyone had arrived while she and Grace were eating their lunch. A patch of sand here and there was barely visible through the multitude of bodies. They made their way cautiously through the maze of people and towels, back to the water's edge, the lazy waves lapping gently at their feet.

Grace, several paces ahead, suddenly stopped, bent over, then turned around, holding a stick in her right hand. She smiled at Eve.

"Oh, found your magic wand, have you?" Eve remarked with a bit more acerbity than she had anticipated.

"As a matter of fact, yes!" she responded.

Eve beheld Grace, smiling unabashedly, triumphantly holding up her thin piece of driftwood. She was standing barefoot in her white flowing sundress, the afternoon sun casting a halo around her features. The ends of her long blonde hair blew around her face with each tease of the wind.

Despite her cynicism about Grace's current tangent, Eve was intrigued and found herself reluctantly smiling back.

Grace turned, continuing their walk. "Do you remember the exercise early this morning where I had you put everything in the shoebox, and you were able to have a direct experience of your soul?"

Eve nodded, remembering.

"Well, *that* is *who you really are*, but, for a moment, I want you to envision *another* you—a you that is full of fear, guilt, pain and hurt. This negativity—which you carry around in your tissues and cells—is a part of your ego and has an energy all its own. I call it the *burden body*. It has a density, a feel, to it, and for many people, it's their constant companion. Like a big panting dog, with its tongue lolling out as it happily sits beside you, you carry this entity around with you wherever you go. That's why getting the new house or the new job or the new relationship doesn't change how you feel about yourself or your life because *that you* comes with you. This burden body is very separate from who you are deep down inside. It can be left behind for good. It's just a matter of choice.

"All the hurt, all the guilt and fear from the past really can disappear just like that." Grace snapped her own fingers to illustrate. "There is a wonderful expression: 'The thoughts you had yesterday make up your today. And the thoughts you have today make up your tomorrow.' Every moment of every day we all have an opportunity to create our experiences, to create the life we want. If we carry negative baggage from the past, all we have to do is make the choice that we don't need it anymore. We keep the wonderful, fun, loving memories and experiences from the past and release all of the negative ones. By realizing that we can literally dump what's not necessary or useful toward our growth at any given moment, we can essentially clean our own slates indefinitely."

Grace stopped abruptly, turning toward Eve. "Back at the deck, I told you that your parents weren't the real problem; your thoughts on the subject were. I realize that hit a nerve, for which I apologize. But if you were living from your soul instead of the ego, if you viewed the situation from the centre of that wheel, you wouldn't be affected emotionally by what your parents did or didn't do, or what they said or didn't say. You see, when you live from your soul, it's not as if the world stops doing what it did previously to trigger you; the situations in your life don't just morph into something 'perfect' and wonderful. Instead, *your entire perception about life changes*. So, even though others may be trying to push your buttons, as far as you're concerned, there are no more buttons to be pushed. Thus, it becomes a fascinating experiment in human nature. As you sit there, observing your parents behaving like they have always behaved, you can shake your head in amazement and move forward without them holding you back any longer."

"I must admit, I have a rather difficult time imagining that I could just sit there listening to my parents' lectures and not be affected by them," Eve remarked.

"Remember when I asked you to remove the past, the guilt, the fear and all the thoughts and associations of your parents' influence on you? When I asked you to imagine a clean slate, with the freedom to be who you wanted to be, to choose what and how you wanted to choose, you told me that you wanted to create, to find your passion again. I want you to remember what it felt like to imagine, even for a moment, that you could be who you've always wanted to be."

Walking toward a large log that had fallen near the edge of the forest that bordered part of the beach, Grace motioned to Eve. "Have a seat, Eve, and close your eyes. There's an exercise that will show you what it can truly feel like when you take away all that baggage."

Since the log was wide enough, Eve decided to lie down, shifting and adjusting her body until she was comfortable. Moving her ponytail over to the side, she pulled her cap a little further down over her face and closed her eyes.

"This exercise is not about justifying the past or minimizing the terrible atrocities and injustices that many of us have experienced in our lives. We want to remove the emotional pain associated with these devastating events so that, for even a moment, we can truly feel what it would be like if all the emotional pain associated with the past could just disappear. The memory does not vanish, and removing the emotion does not minimize the events of the past. The emotion, however, does stop us from feeling a true sense of release, even if that gift of release is something we have deeply craved and desired for many years. No matter how horrible our circumstances, we need to give ourselves permission to feel what it would be like to truly be free of the bondage of the past. So in this exercise, Eve, I want you to release all the pain associated with your past, and watch your soul soar!

"Just like the last exercise, the first thing I'm going to have you do, Eve, is focus on your breath.

"Without using words to describe or create commentary on what is happening, follow your inhale and exhale as it moves rhythmically throughout your body. As you breathe, so does every one of the trillions of cells in your body.

"Try to imagine your entire body breathing with you. Visualize your breath as waves. As you inhale, imagine the wave of your breath rolling to the shore, filling you from your toes all the way up to your fingers, all the way up to the crown of your head. Then, as you exhale, feel the wave flowing away from the shore, and as it does, release the breath from the crown of your head through to your fingertips, down to your toes. Breathe with each wave, filling your body with breath on each inhale, releasing, surrendering your body on each exhale.

"Be aware of every moment of your breath. From the moment the inhale starts, follow it through to its middle and watch as it flows effortlessly into the exhale. Watch the exhale through its middle, and follow it to its end as it flows softly back into the inhale.

"Take a few minutes to connect with your breath. If thoughts come into your mind, don't worry; just let them pass, bringing your awareness back to the waves of your breath.

"If you feel ready, Eve, we can move on to relaxing your body."

From somewhere far away, Eve felt herself nod.

"Good," Grace said. "Now I want you to allow your breath to return to an easy, natural rhythm while I talk you through relaxing your body one muscle at a time. I want you to take all the time you need, moving slowly, visualizing and feeling each part of your body as you start to relax it.

"Allow your unconscious to take control of your breathing—let your body breathe any way it wants, let it go wherever it wants.

"I want you to bring your awareness to your toes. Relax your toes. Relax the top of your feet, the bottom of your feet, even the sides of your feet. Let them fall away from the body. Let them move out any way they want. Then take that feeling of relaxation into your legs. Relax your legs from your ankles all the way up to your knees and then all the way up to your hips.

"Completely relax your abdomen. Don't hold your tummy in. Just let it all go. Relax the muscles throughout your chest and ribcage, feeling the breath move effortlessly throughout the torso. Relax your entire spine. Feel the lower back release, the middle back release and the upper back release.

"Now take your awareness into your fingers. Relax your fingers, the backs of your hands and the palms of your hands. Let go of any gripping or holding in your hands. Feel the relaxation move from your wrists up to your elbows and from your elbows up to your shoulders. Completely relax your shoulders.

"Release any tension in the back of your neck and the sides of your neck. Let your throat soften. Relax your jaw. Soften the muscles around your mouth. Soften the muscles around your eyes. Feel your entire face relax. Release all the muscles throughout your entire scalp.

"I want you to visualize that wave of relaxation moving throughout your whole body. If any area is resisting, just pay extra attention to that part of your body, asking it gently to release and let go."

Eve sighed, her body melting.

"From this luxuriously relaxed perspective, I want you to examine the role of the past in your life. Take a moment and think deeply about your past—all the things that have happened from the moment you were conceived, to all the things that happened only yesterday. What aspects of the past are causing you pain?

"When you hold on to painful images and feelings from or about the past, you become deeply attached to that misery, keeping it buried and locked away inside yourself. You feel engulfed, enslaved to a past filled with negative and painful thoughts and emotions. However, the past, on its own, has no power. It is alive, here in your present, only because your thoughts and your perspective give it continued life. You are going to let go of the negative past completely, finally allowing yourself to move forward with lightness and freedom.

"I want you to once again visualize that shelf in front of you. If you are unable to see a shelf clearly in your mind, just get a sense of it; a feeling of that shelf being there. On that shelf, place another shoebox. In the first box you placed the ego—all of the hats and labels that you mistakenly identified as yourself. In this second box, you are going to place all the pain, the hurt, the guilt and the fear from the past. I really want you to take all the time you need to work through this exercise. Feel, reflect and take in each point without rushing.

"This is not a time to justify wrongdoing, nor is it necessarily about forgiveness. This exercise is about removing the negative emotions and feelings attached to the painful memories and experiences of the past so you can feel the tremendous release that comes from a new, awakened perspective. But if at any time the exercise becomes uncomfortable, I want you to stop, open your eyes and breathe deeply. Feel free to walk away if you need to. You can always try again later, when you feel ready.

"Let's start by removing all the negativity from the past and placing it into the shoebox.

"If you were hurt physically, emotionally or spiritually, place all that hurt into the box. Remove all the emotions and feelings attached to that hurt, all the anger, all the guilt, all the fear and sadness, and place them into the shoebox.

"If you are holding on to feelings of betrayal, place them into the box.

"If you were abused, find all the painful memories and emotions attached to that abuse, lift them from their hiding place, release them from your heart, and place them into the box.

"If you felt abandoned, alone or unwanted, place those painful feelings into the shoebox.

"If you were made to feel worthless, if you were criticized or made to stay silent, put the pain associated with those feelings into the box.

"If you were made to feel shame, take that emotion, take that pain, and place it into the box.

"If you have regrets, place them, and all the emotional heaviness associated with them, into the shoebox.

"If you are weighed down by remorse, lift all the negativity, guilt and doubt from your heart, completely remove it from your body and place it all into the shoebox.

"If you were made to live in fear, afraid to breathe, afraid to live, place all that fear into the shoebox. Place all the hurt and confusion, brought about through constantly questioning and second-guessing yourself, into the box.

"If you were bullied or put down, place that anger and hurt into the shoebox.

"If you were made to doubt your abilities, your worth or your right to live and find happiness, place all that indignation and hurt into the box.

"Remove all your hurt and pain, all your anger and guilt, all the fear and questioning from your heart, your mind and your body. Lift all the negative emotions and feelings from deep within and lighten your entire body. Remove it all and place it into the shoebox.

"Envision all those painful memories and emotions lifted from your body and see them safely secured away into that shoebox. *Feel* how the memories and emotions are no longer a part of you. Sense that they are now completely separate from you.

"Now, as you lie here, you can truly *feel* that all the hurt and pain from the past has been lifted from you and placed into the box. You are here looking at that box, and that box is separate from who you are right now.

"*Feel* the lightness.

"*Feel* the freedom and the peace that comes from letting go of the pain from the past.

"*Feel* how, for the first time in a long time, you are truly free, free and open to new opportunities, free and open to a new peaceful awareness.

"Awaken to a new life, Eve, to a new you!"

Eve opened her eyes. Sensations and her surroundings slowly came back to her. Children squealed in the distance; the warm breeze drifted over her bare arms and legs; a gull cawed overhead. The fresh scent of pine floated from the forest behind her; and the upturned mouth of Grace smiled down at her, clear blue eyes twinkling.

"Well, how did that feel?" Grace inquired.

Eve stretched, taking her time sitting up. "That was amazing! I can't believe how light I feel, as if the weight of the world has been lifted off my shoulders! I mean, not only do I feel lighter emotionally, but physically I even feel a sense of relief and release. It's incredible how freeing that felt!"

"All that hurt and pain gets trapped inside. We become so identified with it that it blinds our ability to move forward in life. We stay emotionally trapped in the past, and because of that, we can never start our future. We just keep living the same cycles, repeating the same old patterns again and again, until we finally let go of the past. After that the patterns stop, and suddenly we find ourselves in a very different place, with opportunities and experiences that we never noticed before."

Tucking her skirt beneath her, Grace sat down beside Eve. "I want you to understand how important reflection, or self-study, is in finding your path to fulfillment. Whenever we question our beliefs, our pain or our choices, we create an opportunity for growth. Change cannot happen without awareness. With awareness we gain *knowledge*, which is power. The more we understand our impulses and what drives us to act in a certain way or say certain things, the more we understand our suffering, and this self-study always leads us to awareness. But even after we have reflected, ruminated, rationalized and talked it through a million different ways, either in our own mind, to a friend or even to a counsellor, eventually we just have to let it all go.

"Eve, you say you know that your parents' guilt trips are causing you a lot of grief. But where has that knowledge gotten you? If you truly want to be free from the past, you have to, on a deeply unconscious level, really let it all go."

She looked intently at Eve. "For a *moment* you let go of all the hurt and guilt associated with the past, and for a *moment* you felt light and free. But how can you truly and completely let it go for good? Do you need to spend the next ten years in silent reflection? Maybe, or perhaps, just perhaps, there is a simpler way."

Standing up, Grace walked toward the water. She turned and flashed a knowing smile at Eve. "This is where my magic wand comes in."

Eve watched in silence as Grace drew a line in the sand with her "magic wand."

"A moment ago, you experienced what it feels like to live without the past holding you back, without the baggage dragging you down, stopping you from living the life you want to live. The only difference between living like that for a *moment* and living like that from *this moment on* is your choice! If you've had enough of the past holding you back, if you've had enough of the guilt and the hurt choking your joy here in the present, it's time to let it go. You can live a life free from the past. You can take all that suffering away, releasing it once and for all. *All you have to do is choose.* Releasing these emotions doesn't trivialize your past, and it doesn't justify others' insufferable actions, but it does allow you to break the cycle of pain and misery that has underscored your efforts to find true happiness and joy. Pain, anger and fear can only continue to hurt you if you let them. They are powerful emotions that, if taken away, no longer have any power over you. If you're tired of feeling pain, if you've had enough of trying to move forward only to be brought back down by your fears and suffering, if you want to change, if you want to finally be rid of all that baggage, if you want to release all that negativity once and for all, all you have to do is make the conscious decision that *enough is enough*. That from this moment on, you will no longer be held back by things that happened in the past; that from this moment on, no matter what atrocities befell you in the past, no matter what indecencies, no matter what indignation, you will no longer be held captive, you will no longer suffer. You will no longer allow the past and those from the past to hold sway over you. You will be free. You will live your life the way you want to live. You will be the person you've always wanted to be."

"I would really like to be able to do that," Eve replied wistfully.

"Then don't let the past hold you back a moment longer, Eve. You are not your past. You do not need the emotional pain from the past to live your life. In fact, you will begin to thrive once you realize that living in the past and letting it control you is what has been holding you back all along. So, if you are ready to move forward, to truly be free, you just have to make the choice to let it all go, to leave it all behind. Put that baggage, that shoebox, into the basket of a giant hot-air balloon, release it into the sky and watch as it gets smaller and smaller, fading farther and farther from sight, until it is just a tiny speck on the horizon. And then, in the blink of an eye, watch as it completely disappears. The choice is yours, Eve—it always has been."

Grace pointed to her left, indicating where Eve was sitting. "On this side of the line, Eve, is the way you've always been and felt, with the negative, emotional past clinging to your heart like an albatross, like a dark, heavy cloak that you must wear wherever you go. On the other side of the line is a new perspective, a new life that comes from making the decision to step across that divide of experiencing *relief for a moment* to experiencing *relief from this moment on*. What do you think, Eve, are you ready to walk across the line?"

Eve rose decisively and walked over to the freshly drawn line in the sand. *Do I want to let the past go? Yes. Absolutely!* To be free of all that emotional pain and guilt was an opportunity she couldn't possibly pass up. She could feel the lightness around her from even just contemplating the prospect. *Who wouldn't want to feel like that from this moment on?* She grinned confidently at Grace and took a big, bold step across the line.

"Well," Grace inquired, "how do you feel, Eve?"

"I'm surprised how simple that was!" Eve shook her head in amazement. "It feels like a profound sense of relief and peace has washed over me. I can't believe that it came down to something as simple as just making a choice!" She stared at the line in the sand, a solid affirmation of a decision, her decision to let the pain go. "I wonder what would have happened if I'd made that choice ten years ago? How different would my life have been?"

"There is a belief that when the student is ready, the teacher will appear. That teacher can appear in the form of a book, a person or an experience. You might not have been ready to learn that lesson ten years ago Eve, but since you were open to the possibility today, you could see how easy the choice was.

"And anyone can do it," Grace added. "All they have to do is find a line they can physically cross. It can be the threshold of their front door, a line on the floor tiles, or a piece of string. If they are truly done with having the past hold them back, all they need to do is take a leap of faith and walk across that line."

Chapter 4

Karmic Awareness

A young family setting up a blanket near the shoreline caught Eve's attention. Three boisterous young boys seemed eager to get into the water and jumped up and down with excitement.

With Grace in step beside her, Eve walked back and sat down on the log, watching as a young woman, most likely the mother, leaned forward, wagging her finger at the tallest of the boys, her face stern. He nodded, and then all three boys raced into the lake, kicking up and splashing water around them.

Within moments, the tallest boy splashed water on the smallest child's face. The young child unleashed a torrent of cries and appeals that Eve could hear from where she sat. This resulted in the mother storming over and reprimanding him. No sooner had she turned away when the middle boy came exploding out of the water, sputtering and coughing. She spun around and pointed her finger at the tallest boy and then at the blanket. The child protested, waving his arms and shaking his head. She stood firm, and eventually he stomped over and plopped down onto the blanket, pouting, his arms crossed over his chest.

Eve chuckled, giving Grace a friendly nudge with her elbow. "That reminds me of my two boys."

"It looks as though he has learned a valuable lesson," Grace offered.

"Oh, if only it were that simple," Eve mused.

Sweeping her hands through the air, Grace gestured. "Life is an intricate, exquisite tapestry where the threads of consequence and free will magically weave their eternal lessons."

"That was very poetic," Eve admitted.

"Thank you," Grace said, smiling. "On a simpler note, we all have lessons to learn. In fact, we are learning continually, whether we are conscious of it or not. Through the use of our free will, we make choices, and there are consequences to everything we say, think and do! When we live through the ego, those consequences provide us with the lessons we must learn.

"Absolutely everything is a result of consequence. The fact that we, as human beings, exist at all is a consequence of the Big Bang, a planet being the right distance from its sun, our ancient ancestors' biological will to survive and thrive, and our parents' individual involvement in our manifestation. Ever since time began, there have been consequences. Every thought, every action, every word ever spoken has had repercussions in the web of life.

"Imagine life as a locomotive travelling at the speed of light. It is propelled forward by the consequences of everything that has come before. Everything has already been set in motion by all the events of the past. Then you, at the moment of your birth, decide to catch that train at that particular moment in time and space."

Grace studied Eve closely. "You have been altering the world around you since your conception. And the lessons you must learn on this journey are based on the consequences of that interaction. We've already discussed the idea that our past experiences alter our view of the present. Do you remember when I spoke about the ego, with its sunglasses and filters?"

"Yes, you mentioned the ego distorts or discolours our reality, or the way we perceive things," Eve responded.

"Exactly. All the things we have seen, heard, smelled, tasted and felt have left an indelible impression on the ego and therefore affect how we perceive the world.

"Basically, we take all our scholarly learning and all our behavioural learning—those tribal beliefs we garnered from interacting with our parents, friends, teachers, etc.—and we create a stew of opinions, biases, judgments and expectations of the world and people around us. We then think, speak and act under that strong influence. The lessons we must learn in life are based on the decisions we make while eating that stew … with our sunglasses on!"

Eve stared at Grace for a moment. "Okay, let me see if I've got this straight. You're telling me that everything that has ever happened is a result of consequences in one form or another."

"That's right."

"And that everything I've ever done has also created consequences, like throwing a rock into a pond creates a ripple effect."

"Absolutely! And you never know what effect those ripples will have."

"Okay, I see that. But you're also telling me that the ego creates these ripples, these consequences. Why is that so important?"

"Well, if you are making decisions and acting from the ego, which is only interested in itself and keeps you separate and suffering by filling you with judgments and biases, can you imagine what the consequences, the effects, of that type of behaviour will have on the world? Not to mention the effects of that influence on you? Then imagine a different type of ripple, the kind that comes from acting from compassion, love and peace. The effects of *that* type of vibration or action will send a very different signal out into the world, thereby attracting love, peace and compassion back in your direction.

"There is a wonderful sentiment: If you were to consider every thought you have—of which you have tens of thousands a day, by the way—as an act of prayer, and that each prayer was always answered … whether good or bad, would you reconsider what you thought about? If you can grasp the significance of that concept, it will give you an indication of how our thoughts, words and actions affect us and those around us."

"I see." Eve did. She could clearly see the difference and realized that perhaps she wasn't sending or receiving the best messages. Some of the time she knew she was sending out "good vibrations," as the Beach Boys so aptly put it, but on other occasions when she wasn't happy or was dwelling on the past or some other injustices, she could sense the magnitude of influence that her behaviour might have on others … and even on herself.

"The beauty in all this, though," Grace continued, "is that we always have a choice. We have a choice in what we think, what we say, what we do, and ultimately, what we project into the world. That's where our free will comes in.

"So, to use your past interactions with your parents as an example, every decision you've made, Eve, was yours to make and yours alone. Not your parents'—yours. They may complain, berate, and in general give you a run for your money, but a decision to stand your ground and choose your art versus returning to school to upgrade your degree is ultimately *your* decision to make. You've always had free will, Eve—free will to make decisions and choices every moment of your life. We all do."

"I must admit, sometimes it sure didn't feel that way," Eve grumbled.

"We always have a choice, Eve, even if it's just *how we choose to feel* about something in our mind.

"Some of us have had terrible atrocities devastate our lives, and physically we may not have had the opportunity to escape a situation, but we do have power over our thoughts; we can choose to think differently about our misfortune. It is an attitude adjustment that requires effort—we use our free will to change our state of mind. Although it may be difficult to find a way to cope and endure trauma while directly in the midst of experiencing it, we need to know that when the danger has passed, we can make a choice to move through it instead of holding onto the feelings and pains associated with those events long after they have happened. We can choose to let the past go and *thrive* in the present, rather than just survive."

"I don't know how anybody could do that," Eve said as she looked in the direction of the water. The three boys were now laughing and playing without a care in the world, running around the beach, batting and kicking a red-and-white-striped beach ball.

"It's more common than you might think. We are all capable of overcoming hardship. Some people can endure horrific tragedies, yet they come through them stronger, with a powerful sense of purpose— Nelson Mandela is a compelling example. After engaging in anti-apartheid activities in South Africa, Mandela was convicted and sentenced to a life in prison. For twenty-seven years he toiled in hard physical labour. But during his imprisonment, he gained worldwide support for his firm stance against racial discrimination and was subsequently released. He received a Nobel Peace Prize for his efforts and was eventually elected the first black president of South Africa!

"He could have stewed and lamented his fate while he laboured in the lime quarries, but he chose instead to focus on his goal of a multiracial democracy. He chose not to let his circumstances defeat him!

"People like Mandela take the very difficult circumstances of their lives and choose to think of them as catalysts for change, finding empowerment, strength and courage as they conquer and overcome their adversities. Others do not.

"What makes those who triumph over obstacles so different from those who don't? Nothing. They simply made a choice that they *would not* allow that negativity to dominate their lives.

"This may seem like an insensitive thing to say to all those who are struggling and suffering in their lives. But if you tried to look instead at the *hope* in that statement, you would see that anyone, regardless of how stuck in the mud they feel they are, no matter how low or how hurt they are, can find their way out of pain, because if one person can overcome hardship and adversity, then it's possible for others to follow. And the path to that salvation is *choice*."

Grace walked over to the water's edge. Picking up a rock, she skipped it across the lake's glassy surface. Eve rose to join her and hunted along the beach for a good skipping stone. When she found the perfect specimen of smooth, glossy black slate, she flicked her wrist and sent the stone skipping across the water, counting each hop until it sank and disappeared.

"The most powerful choice we have is how we perceive things. For example, if we cannot see that we have a choice to view a very difficult situation differently, how can we change? How can we break the cycle of suffering? We are left with the same ripples coming back to us again and again, the same patterns in our lives, the same difficulties and struggles." Grace sent another stone whipping across the water. The small ripples caused by the stone sent shimmering waves back toward the shore, to where they were standing.

"We need to be aware of the fact that we always have a choice! We always have the choice to make a new decision; therefore, we always have the choice to alter our consequences. We always have the opportunity to send a new ripple out into the world, to change our situation and our circumstances by simply choosing to view our situation differently by making the necessary changes to our thoughts. Awareness is essential to end suffering. When it comes to consequences, we must become aware of and understand the cycles that our decisions and actions constantly set in motion."

Eve thought about that for a moment. "I guess it's like the boy who was reprimanded and told to get out of the water—his choices led to an unsavoury consequence, which perhaps will make him more aware of his actions in the future."

Grace nodded. "Every thought, word and action has a corresponding consequence. At some point in our journey we will be confronted by the effects of those ripples. And if those ripples or consequences originated from the ego, then they contain lessons for us to learn from, lessons otherwise known as karma. That young boy learned his lesson rather quickly." Grace winked as she turned to walk back toward the log. Eve followed, sitting down.

Picking up her magic wand, Grace drew a pattern of intersecting lines in the sand. "As we move through life, two elaborate patterns are fundamental to our conscious experience. One is made by karma; the other is made by our soul.

"When a weaver sits down to create fabric, the warp, the vertical threads, are held taut by the loom. The weaver, using a shuttle, weaves the horizontal threads, the weft, over and under, in and out, around the stationary warp. The weft must alter its course to manoeuvre around the rigid warp, just as karma, the rigid warp, presents each of us with obstacles that provide us with unique lessons—the consequences that arise out of each and every thought, action and word spoken through the ego in our lifetime.

"Our soul, on its joyful path as the weft, weaves through and around, learning from each obstacle in its path. Every moment we must learn from the consequences of the past as we pursue a life of happiness and fulfillment. Our success in overcoming those obstacles and learning from the past determines whether or not we find true happiness. This is the primordial dance between karma and our soul, and it has shaped the fabric of life since time immortal."

"I've heard the word *karma* before, but I never quite understood it," Eve said, considering Grace's imagery.

Grace smiled. "Every obstacle in your life is a lesson. Every experience you are having or have had is a lesson that you must learn. Every moment of every day, you experience and assimilate what is happening around you. What you take away and learn from those situations constitutes the lessons you are here to learn.

"The whole purpose for having these obstacles and lessons is to expand our consciousness and find lasting happiness, which will *only* happen if we are *aware* of our patterns—aware of the fact that we are constantly making ripples and receiving back their effects. Then we need to make informed choices that help us to feel good about ourselves and our lives. Being aware of our patterns and the effects and consequences that they continually generate and making choices that no longer manifest an undesirable outcome will happen effortlessly when we are living from our soul.

"Typically, however, we are not aware of our patterns because we are living in the ego. When we live from the perspective of the ego, our interactions are driven by behaviour that is unaware and unconscious or repetitive and reactive—our typical knee-jerk reactions. When the ego influences us with its myriad opinions and judgments, we rarely think about what is driving our reactions. We live on the outside of that wooden wagon wheel and just react to whatever comes our way. This type of behaviour leads us to make uninformed, often unwise, even unhealthy choices, which in turn leads to unfavourable consequences. In such cases, we have not learned our lessons, and therefore we experience the *unfavourable* consequence of repeating similar scenarios in the karmic cycle of suffering over and over again until we get it right. Plus, with karma's diligent efforts trying to teach us our lessons, each repetition will up the ante, so to speak, making the lessons more difficult—not to decipher necessarily, but more difficult to handle. We may find ourselves experiencing situations that elicit increasingly emotional, energetic reactions. The key is to recognize that the universe will never give us more than we can handle. It may be very difficult to appreciate that when we feel we are in the midst of chaos and suffering, a common state of affairs whilst we are living in the ego."

"Difficult indeed," Eve replied with an edge of sarcasm. "I would never have guessed that the universe was only giving me as much as I could handle, because honestly, sometimes I've felt completely overwhelmed."

"Some challenges can be very difficult. That's why it's important to recognize and know where our choices are coming from. It's essential to start making decisions from our soul, rather than reacting through the ego. When we abide in our soul, we approach every situation with awareness, which gives us the opportunity to make an informed choice. We choose to break a particular cycle of suffering because we can see what will happen if we react the way we always do. Consequently, with our informed, wise choice, we react differently to the situation, rather than continuing the customary reactions from the ego, thus escaping the trap of falling back into the cycle of our programmed tendencies. This creates *favourable* consequences; in other words, we get to move on because we have broken that specific, karmic cycle."

"Ever since I made the decision to stay at home and put my career on hold, I've had to listen to my parents' lectures and relentless criticism. I always end up feeling upset, frustrated and guilty, unable to say how I really feel." Eve picked up a rock and threw it toward the water. It missed. She frowned. She turned her attention back to Grace. "But you're telling me that if I want a favourable consequence, I need to learn how to react differently to my 'difficult'"—she bent two fingers on each hand, making a pair of quotation marks—"parents? I love them, but they haven't made my life easy."

"Yes. In order to create a favourable consequence, you need to be aware of your choices and change your thoughts, words, and actions when you interact with your parents. Your reactions, thus far, have been unconscious—you haven't been aware of the conditioned patterns you've been repeating. When most people react to parents, friends, spouses, children, co-workers, bosses—you name it—if they are controlled by the ego, they rely on conditioned, pre-programmed responses, which automatically cause them to reenact the same parts in their continuing daily dramas. In similar situations, they always play the same part.

"What if our spouse or significant other comes to us to discuss finances? We may find ourselves resorting to our programmed reactions and experiencing emotions and feelings that always arise whenever finances are brought up. Perhaps we're always defensive; perhaps we always go on the offensive; perhaps we always feel victimized or controlled or move into denial, or we always feel we have to justify our position."

Eve considered that for a moment. "You know what? Now that I think of it, I always get stressed whenever Tom wants to talk about money. I feel controlled, and I feel like I always have to go on the defensive, justifying every little thing I do. But I know that's not fair. He's not accusing or judging me. In fact, he never interferes with how I spend our money, but I can't help reacting the way I do. Why do I do that?"

"Why do we always react in the exact same way each time the same trigger appears? That's a good question, Eve. It's because we are unaware of the situation, unaware that the same situation continually occurs in our lives, and unaware that we are, in fact, reacting in the exact same way each and every time. And the way to stop those knee-jerk reactions and break the karmic cycle is through awareness."

Chapter 5

Ruts

Grace pointed to a trail marker off to the left. "Would you like to take a walk through the forest up to the dunes?" she asked.

Eve looked behind her. "Sure, sounds like fun." She reached into her bag and pulled out her sandals. "Should we put on some bug spray?" she wondered, looking at her bare legs and arms.

"I don't know? *Should we?*" Grace repeated. "Sounds like you are drifting off into another one of your unconscious repetitive patterns with that *should*."

Standing, Eve shook her head. "Wow, how do you do that?" She laughed.

"You just have to become more aware of what you say, think and do." Grace motioned to Eve to follow, and they headed toward the trail, the dense vegetation quickly closing in around them.

"The thing about repetitive, reactive behaviours is that over time they become deeply ensconced in our physiology. By always reacting a certain way to a certain stimulus, we create deep, neural pathways, deep ingrained ruts. We have absolutely no concept that we are doing so. We become very comfortable living unconsciously, reacting to everything and everyone without thinking it through or examining its presence in our lives. These patterns of behaviours or reactions become so habitual that we carpet our ruts, set up walls, buy wonderful furniture and move in. Eventually, over time, as these repetitive reactions continue, we forget that we have built a foundation on a rut and are unable to discern its original cause—why we began reacting like that in the first place. Keep in mind that most of our repetitive reactions were created through our original interactions with our tribes, as far back as our conception. These reactions accumulated and deeply entrenched themselves into our psyche. We could spend years searching, but it's not necessary to understand the root cause of our behaviours. It doesn't matter if our parents are the underlying cause of any of our ruts; we just need to be *aware* that there is a pattern, a rut, hiding under that carpet. And we have to use our free will to decide that we no longer want it there, that we no longer want it influencing our lives!

"In order to do this, we need to change our thoughts! Ruts are ingrained habits of thinking that keep us reacting, stuck deep in an unwanted or undesirable situation or *cloud* of thinking."

The peaceful silence of the forest was suddenly interrupted by the shrill cawing of a crow calling a warning as Grace and Eve passed the winged sentry guarding its territory. The cawing was answered by several more cries, and a flurry of leaves rustled as a dozen birds took flight.

"Oh, that startled me." Eve pressed her hand over her pounding heart. She looked up into the canopy and promptly fell forward when she tripped over an exposed tree root.

"Are you all right?" Grace asked, extending her hand.

"I'm fine," Eve said, accepting Grace's hand. She righted herself and brushed the dirt from her shorts.

Grace removed a leaf from Eve's hair. "You know, someone once said to me, 'It's not about getting to the top of the mountain and staying there, it's *all* about how quickly you can pick yourself up and dust yourself off.' At first, that concept seems reasonable enough, but that's exactly why we continue to stay stuck in our ruts. We are unaware that 'here we go again' is playing out in our lives' dramas. And rather than lifting ourselves up and out of our programmed thoughts, behaviours and reactions, once and for all, *finally* staying at the top of the mountain—the top being happiness and fulfillment, where we all want to *be*—we resign ourselves to falling right back into that same situation, that same rut, again and again."

They resumed their walk, Eve keeping a wary eye on the terrain.

"One of the many tribal beliefs that we are raised on is the repetitive pattern of 'try, try, try again,' like *The Little Engine That Could,* but the problem is, *we keep trying the same things.* We need to become aware of our patterns so that we can change our thoughts and programmed behaviours, thus filling in our ruts.

"When we react to people or situations and then dwell on them, running the situation over and over in our minds, we allow the pattern to continue by fuelling our negative emotions, such as feelings of injustice, fear, anger, guilt, etc. Essentially, we grab hold of the shovel and start digging our ruts even deeper and deeper. We are all really good at this. We will call our friends or family and go on a tirade about how we were wronged or how bad life is or how horrible someone just treated us. We will keep the high-voltage charge of the situation alive and well for days, weeks, months—even years—especially if the emotions and negative self-talk is strong enough and relentless. This is extremely *counterproductive*, by the way."

"'Round and 'round the mulberry bush," Eve sang.

"Exactly. Ruts are not only deeply entrenched neural pathways formed from repetitive behaviours and thoughts, but, like the replaying of those injustices in our mind, where we grab that shovel and start digging, they become the *physical* manifestation of those thoughts and behaviours as they present themselves in our lives."

"Okay, hold on a minute—you've completely lost me."

"Well, let's say you've wanted to lose weight for quite some time. But you have deep neural pathways, deeply entrenched thoughts and behaviours that cause you to act in a self-sabotaging manner. You find yourself not exercising, making poor food choices and maybe even binging when you get stressed. Because you think you are overweight, you physically do things to confirm and reinforce that belief in your mind, causing a great deal of emotional strife in the process. You become stuck in the rut of being overweight.

"If we think something long enough and hard enough, dwelling on it, then our lives start to mirror our projections. We all get into ruts— situations where we feel stuck and unhappy, unable to move beyond our current crisis or circumstances. They are built upon our repetitive thoughts and pent-up emotions. The intensity and magnitude of our emotional responses determine how deep our ruts become. Depression is a good indication of a really deep rut. We know we are depressed but can't seem to lift ourselves up out of our depression, our negativity. Or perhaps we don't even realize we are down again because those feelings of weariness and sadness are such constant companions.

"If we are able to release the charge of our negative emotions, we may climb up out of the trenches of our ruts with barely a nick. However, if we are unable to release our pent-up emotions, we will be stuck, wallowing in our ruts, feeling depleted and helpless as we continue to get dragged down by the undertow of our misery and negative, mental cacophony."

Eve stopped momentarily to look at Grace. "I can relate to that. I've been there—trapped in my own negative thoughts, my mind constantly nattering at me. It's not a good place to be."

"At some point, we *all* reach the bottom of our tolerance, that threshold where we feel we are as low as we can possibly go," Grace continued. They resumed their walk. "For some, that bottom is so low they may feel that they are going to crack under the pressure, thus succumbing to life's external stresses. That is a very dangerous, sensitive time, where we are left with no hope, no will to survive, and no desire to carry on. We all have a different threshold; while some may fall into the pit of despair, others will not.

"Many people on life's path will reach those depths and use them as a catalyst for change. Eventually, deciding that *enough is enough*, they make the changes necessary in their thought process and their perspective to enable them to climb up out of their ruts. Others may be stuck wandering around the catacombs of their tormented minds for their entire lives, never fully happy, never fully at peace, always yearning for something better. They lack the energy, desire and motivation necessary to leave the *comfort* of their ruts, the *comfort* of their own melancholy. This concept, that somehow we choose the comfort of misery over the prospect of happiness, is difficult to accept."

"Why would anyone do that to themselves? I can't see any comfort in being miserable," Eve commented.

"I agree with your sentiment, Eve. However, we quite simply prefer a certain state of mind because we are used to it; it's comfortable. A negative state of mind, such as misery, becomes our constant companion, empowering our shadow self, the Dr. Jekyll to our Mr. Hyde. That shadow self, the burden body, the manifestation of our negativity, is weighted and heavy, but it suits us; it fits us like a glove. We have become very accustomed to its shape, to its feel. Our cells and tissues hold onto that negativity with incredible tenacity. Even if it becomes tattered or torn, filthy and threadbare, many of us will wear that glove well past its demise, just because we are comfortable with its familiarity.

"The ego, the shadow self or burden body, demands a lot of energy and will do whatever it takes—constant negative self-talk, constant refusal to change our moods, etc.—in order to keep the ball in its court. The ego needs energy to survive. It needs fuel to maintain its sense of self, its sense of existence. Negative internal self-talk, which is the constant dialogue of the ego, keeps us stuck in our ruts and fuels our shadow self. It keeps our body weighted with the pressure of our burdens. It needs to be discarded—once and for all!"

"That sounds like a pretty formidable undertaking. How on earth am I supposed to do that?" Eve wanted to know.

"Imagine a small child on the playground. She is being taunted and teased because her name is funny or her nose is too long or perhaps she wears braces and glasses. Kids can be awfully cruel and can throw out some pretty nasty verbal abuse. Perhaps it even escalates to physical abuse. Everything they say to her, every judgment they pin on her, becomes a scarlet letter. If our parents or our teachers and friends were judgmental, each attack or opinion left a scar on our psyche, and even though those childhood voices have all stopped, as adults, we take up the slack. We develop the powerful ability, with our negative self-talk, to berate ourselves and undermine our self-esteem and self-worth, better than any external bully ever could. We continue to replay those old, hurtful labels and judgments in our present, becoming our own worst enemies! But how relevant are those old judgments? Did we really deserve them as children? There we were, trying to live our unique lives, but others came up to us and told us we were bad or ugly or fat or bossy or worthless. That is the realm of limiting beliefs."

Eve scoffed. "My parents have accused me of being selfish, stubborn and inconsiderate. But I didn't realize I've been holding on to those labels, replaying them in my mind like a sadistic merry-go-round."

"What we need to understand is that judgments are the verbalized poisons oozing from the scars of the burden bodies of those who are doing the judging. *It is never personal. We cannot take their backlash personally!* They were acting from *their* pain, lashing out and incinerating everything in their paths. Some judgments were made unconsciously; others were not, meaning that they knew that they were being cruel. Others were just so miserable or so lost within their own negative thoughts that they didn't even realize how hurtful they were being. The point is not to justify or even give a moment's thought to their intentions or their motives.

"When you released the influence of the past—which you did earlier when you crossed the line, Eve—you gave up the need to *understand* why your parents did what they did. The point is to no longer carry their hurtful words and judgments with you into your present life, into the present moment, because holding onto their malicious opinions and negativity maintains their power, their hold over you. This keeps you firmly entrenched in your ruts because you just keep acting the way they told you, you would, or you just keep being the person they told you, you were. You need to take away that power, irrevocably. You need to turn off the negative, self-limiting behaviour that keeps you from reaching your fullest potential. You need to discard those limiting beliefs once and for all. Eve, you need to fill in your ruts!"

"Pass me the shovel!" Eve exclaimed, watching as the dappled sunlight created a golden mosaic across the forest floor.

Grace snorted with mirth. "Well, maybe not a physical shovel, but this is where karma, our lessons, comes in. With our free will and choice to finally respond, '*Enough is enough,*' we can release the emotional attachment to the past and break our karmic patterns once and for all, thus filling in our ruts. And how do we know it's a karmic pattern? Quite simply because we keep encountering the same situation or lesson over and over again. Maybe we were told we were useless as a child, and we, with our self-limiting mental attacks, have kept that *truth* alive and well all our lives.

"Karma will happily provide us with plenty of situations and scenarios where we can *feel* useless, where we *seem* to be fulfilling that *belief.* Until one day, a situation arises that is just so difficult and so emotionally intense that we scream, 'I am *not* useless!', finally altering our *reaction* to the situation. We discover our sense of power, and we tell that good-for-nothing so-and-so in our lives that we are more than capable of handling this, thank you very much. We become totally invigorated. Energy rushes into and through our body; we feel light and vindicated. We have finally filled in our rut! We have finally broken that karmic cycle!"

They rounded a bend in the trail. Mountains of golden sand reached into an azure sky. "We are given many situations in our lives that teach us very powerful lessons, like learning to find our personal power, our courage or patience; learning how to open ourselves to vulnerability— truly opening our heart to others, learning to feel worthy and loved, and to feel safe and supported. There are as many lessons as there are obstacles." Grace smiled. "But they are not always easy to discern."

"Well, I can see how it would be almost impossible to try to find that kind of depth in our everyday circumstances. I mean, I don't go around questioning everything that happens to me to try and find some deeper meaning to it all. I just try to get through the messy stuff still intact," Eve reasoned as she stumbled up the dune's steep slope, her feet sliding, handfuls of hot sand slipping through her fingers.

"That's because you are still living on the outside of the wheel," Grace explained. She lifted her skirt above her knees and joined Eve in the climb. "There is a wonderful poem by Portia Nelson called 'An Autobiography in Five Short Chapters,' where she speaks about a deep hole in the sidewalk.

"In the first chapter, she explains that we walk along a street. There is a deep hole in the sidewalk, and we fall in. We didn't know it was there, and it's certainly not our fault that we fell in, but once inside, we are lost and confused, and it takes us forever to get back out.

"This is akin to our ruts. At first, we are unaware of the cyclical nature of the circumstances that keep repeating in our lives. This lack of awareness is the hole in the sidewalk. When we are faced with an experience that wishes to teach us a lesson—feeling worthy, for example—we are given a scenario in which we would typically feel *unworthy*. Because we didn't see it coming, we are devastated by the situation and feel stuck and helpless. It takes forever to build the willpower necessary to brush ourselves off, pick ourselves up and clamour out of that deep hole, that deep rut."

Eve lost her footing and slid down the steep incline, an avalanche of golden grains on her heels. "Be right there!" she called up, resuming the arduous ascent.

When Eve caught up to Grace, they continued together, giggling, sliding and climbing their way up to the top. Out of breath, they plopped themselves down on the summit, taking a moment to regain their composure as they congratulated themselves on their impeccable climbing skills.

"Where were we?" Grace asked. "Oh, yes—the second chapter. Because we don't realize there is an alternative, we stick to what we know, to what's familiar, and walk down that same street again, with that same deep hole in the middle. This time when we fall in, we cannot believe we are back in the same hole again! It's still not our fault, because we didn't think we would fall into it a second time.

"So, as far as our ruts go, this illustrates how we are thrust into a situation that is becoming familiar—perhaps it's a new relationship with a partner or a new work opportunity. We can see that it has many of the same trappings of some of the previous situations when we have felt unworthy in the past, but because we cannot recognize the pattern and see that we have been there before, this time we are certain that things will be different. When they aren't, when they work out in exactly the same way, it only confirms our sense of worthlessness. Moreover, it still takes a tremendous amount of effort to pick ourselves up and dust ourselves off … again."

"Kind of like climbing this dune!" Eve interjected.

Grace smiled. "Yes, very similar," she agreed, brushing sand off the hem of her dress. "In the third chapter, we are walking down that same familiar street, only this time we see the hole in the sidewalk. Yet again we fall in, because now it's become a habit. We are completely aware that we have fallen into the same trap. Since we now recognize the pattern that has allowed us to fall in once more, it's easier to get out.

"In other words, we see the danger signs posted ahead. We know full well that if we continue to take the current path, it will end precisely the same way it always does, but we plough ahead anyway, as if willing the cosmos to hasten our lesson. We fall in … again. However, this time we are much better prepared, knowing at least how we got there in the first place. We decide that we *can't keep doing this anymore,* that we no longer want to feel worthless, and we pull ourselves up out of our funk much faster. The recovery is much quicker; our wallowing in our ruts and self-misery doesn't last as long because we were ready for this one."

"Okay, I think I'm getting this. Is it like when you spoke about being overweight? I see the Twinkie, I know it's bad for me, and I will feel horrible and 'worthless' in the morning for eating it, but I can't seem to stop myself."

"Exactly. In the fourth chapter, we walk down the same street with that pesky hole still in the sidewalk, but this time we walk around it.

"This is where, presented with the opportunity to fall into our old beliefs, behaviours and habitual way of thinking, into our comfy ruts, we decide *enough is enough,* and we choose instead to follow the path to fulfillment, which will lead to growth, happiness and feelings of self-worth. We finally recognize the patterns that have been holding us back. As a result, we walk around the hole with our head held high.

"In the fifth and final chapter, we walk down a different street. We've learned our lesson, and the consequence of finally closing the chapter on that karmic cycle is a renewed sense of self-worth. We are presented with new opportunities for growth and success and an influx of powerful energy, as the blockages that held us back are finally released. We are at the top of the mountain!" She patted the sand beside her. "No need to start over again—we made it!"

"I think I've been in an awful lot of ruts in my life!" Eve commented. "My reactions to the finances and my parents would mean I'm probably still in around chapter three," she confessed. "I know I need to believe in myself and my decisions, and yet every time my parents discuss my future, it's like I'm ten years old again, unable to defend myself or stand up for myself and who I am. It's really frustrating! Man, I am such a wimp!" she said in dismay.

Chapter 6

You Are Not Who You Think You Are

From their lofty perch, Eve could see an array of sailboats and motor boats dotting the lake. Off in the distance, a lighthouse stood sentry on a jetty of deserted rock that reached out into the choppy waters. At this height, the sounds from the beach disappeared. Only the wind and the occasional call of sea gulls disrupted the serenity around them.

After a few moments, Grace began to laugh. "I can't believe what you just said a few minutes ago. That was quite a mouthful, especially the part about being a wimp! That, my friend, is a very limiting belief."

"Well, it's true. I should be better at standing up for myself. You even told me that earlier."

"What I said earlier was that your parents are not in charge of your decisions, you are, and your *should* has pulled you right back into that tribal mindset, which is just another limiting belief.

"A limiting belief is a programmed mindset, an automatic, habitual way of thinking that we use to define ourselves, but that definition is based on our past experiences and the influence of other people's opinions, judgments and labels—it's not who we really are.

"We accept those labels, judgments, opinions and assumptions from others and *believe* that they are true, using them to define who we think we are. Eve, you have heard things in the past that have precipitated the idea that you are 'a wimp,' so you have placed this label upon yourself and now believe it. False impressions like these reinforce our beliefs in our *perceived* limitations. *Since these limitations are perceived, they are completely false!* We have everything we need to be whoever we want to be, to do whatever we want to do. However, somewhere along the way our experience has taught us otherwise; someone, or several someones, have introduced the notion and then reinforced the idea that somehow we are less. We came into this world complete and whole. We already had all the charm, charisma, drive, personal power, motivation and will to succeed. We already had all the beauty, love, self-esteem, joy, compassion and self-confidence to make all our dreams come true. But then *they* got a hold of us! Parents, peers, bullies, government, authority figures, teachers, media, etc., influenced *who we think we are* with their criticism, attention, punishment, praise, opinions, beliefs, prejudices, judgments and rules."

Picking up a handful of sand, Eve let it sift through her fingers. "Before today, I never considered where my opinions, beliefs and judgments came from. I can't believe how much I am affected by everyone else!"

"It's amazing to realize how much our past influences us. When we spoke earlier about our tribal beliefs, how we like our eggs, I was referring to the concept that our tribes influence us by deciding for us what or who we *should* like or dislike and what we *should* say, think and do. This is extremely limiting. Because in order to feel *accepted* or *loved*, we feel the need to fit into their rigid, tiny little boxes, to conform to their *perfect* image. As we go about our lives, we come in contact with a multitude of people who have opinions about us, either good or bad, thus helping us to further shape the image we have about ourselves in our minds. Then, depending on what other experiences we have in life, we continue to shape and mold ourselves based on our outcomes of success or failure—'I can't do math, that's why I stopped taking it in high school,' or 'I'm never going to get this job; every job interview I've gone to in the past three months has resulted in failure.'

"Each one of these concepts: our tribal influences, the outcomes of our past experiences, and the labels and judgments from others all add up to some pretty limiting beliefs. After all, if we think we are going to fail, why even bother trying? If our tribe has the expectation that women do not work outside the home, or that real men don't cry, think of all the opportunities we may miss or the feelings and fears we may have to hold inside.

"But our tribe's expectations are just that ... our tribe's, not our own. At least they do not have to be! Be open to questioning your reasons for accepting something at face value just because someone has said it is so. Do *you* really feel that way? Do *you* really think that is true? Take the assumptions revolving around the birth of a child. This event is viewed differently depending on the culture into which the baby is born. To some, every newborn baby comes into this world sinning and unworthy, all because of a snake and an apple, whereas in other cultures, each baby enters this world perfect and beautiful. Quite a contrast! We can see that such ideas, right from the start, influence how we view and feel about ourselves and how *we had absolutely nothing at all to do with them in the first place*. Neither perspective or philosophy is right or wrong. It just illustrates how our tribal beliefs influence our behaviours and thoughts, and if any of the tribe's opinions or views conflict with our own individual sense of understanding and experience, then perhaps it's time to question their presence in our lives."

"I really need to learn how to do that," Eve acknowledged. "To check in with myself, to determine how *I* really feel about something and whether it is true for *me*, rather than accepting it at face value just because someone said so, or because it has always been that way."

"Labels, judgments and opinions from others are also subject to scrutiny. They have nothing to do with us personally. Yet whether we hear them once or repeatedly, we take them onto ourselves and own them as truth. I know we spoke about this earlier, but when we relive the haunting memories of those children taunting us on the playground, or recall something our parents said to us, or when we receive and interpret messages from the media— labels and judgments like 'I'm stupid,' 'I'm ugly,' 'I'm fat,' 'I'm a loser,' 'No one loves me,' 'I'm all alone,' 'No one cares about me,' 'Everybody hates me,' 'I have no friends,' 'I'm worthless,' etc.—become a part of our identity—who we *think* we are. But those labels and judgments are not our own; they are the poisons, toxins and unequivocally tainted viewpoints of the opinionated person or persons doing the judging and labelling."

"Like when I called myself a wimp." Eve watched a gull circle down toward the water. "I can see how judgments placed upon me by my 'tribe,' as you put it, have influenced and often undermined my self-confidence."

Grace leaned back on her elbows, stretching her legs out in the soft golden sand. "The realm of confidence can be a formidable limiting belief. If you do not feel confident, you will hold yourself back. Think of all the things you didn't do because you believed you were a 'wimp.' If that belief hadn't impeded you, you might have attempted something new.

"Our internal opinions create our *belief of confidence*—if we believe we have limitations, it affects our ability or willingness to do something. Our confidence in our ability to do, or not to do, something is what determines our position on the matter—are we able or unable to do it? This will either hold us back or allow us to move forward. To give you an idea of how confidence in our abilities influences our actions, let's take something as simple as learning how to walk. At first, we watched everyone else around us. We studied and observed their movements and mannerisms. Then, we reached a certain level of confidence to at least attempt that first cautious step. If we fell, it probably dampened our confidence for a time, but as we continued to watch everyone else walking around, eventually we got up the nerve to try it again. Let's say this time we were successful. We managed to take a step toward the toy. We were very focused and extremely pleased with ourselves. Perhaps we even received a fanfare, praising our ability. The point is, this particular experiment was a success, so we began to build confidence in our ability to walk. The more we practised, the more we were able to walk, until we were so confident, we didn't need to think about it anymore; we didn't second-guess our ability. We just *knew* we could walk, and that was that. We were off and running, so to speak." Grace chuckled.

"And it's a good thing, too, or we would all still be crawling, though in saying that, I think we did more crawling than walking trying to get up this dune." Eve laughed. "But seriously, it's not always easy to build up confidence."

"Confidence in our abilities is the realm of the ego. We need to try things out again and again until we form an opinion as to whether or not we are good at this or bad at that, and it all depends on how many times we fail or succeed, which determines our *belief* on the subject. This constant experimentation throughout all areas of our lives—relationships, work, sports, etc.—defines our *belief* in ourselves and our abilities. Through trial and error, we create a picture in our mind of our strengths and weaknesses. Our *belief of confidence* can be very limiting. If we are confident we can do something, we will usually attempt it, but if we are not confident, we typically hang back, too uncertain and anxious to even make an attempt.

"And by belief of confidence, I mean exactly that. Confidence is something we *tell ourselves to believe in.* If we threw away the concept of confidence entirely, completely wiped the slate clean, and gave ourselves every opportunity to try something new with the enthusiasm, hope and wonder of a child, we would amaze ourselves with our own potential and abilities. But since we *believe* we can or can't do something because of our experiences in the past, that opinion becomes part of our constant background noise, the incessant cacophony of the ego, and just another limiting belief.

"What we need to understand is that just because something happened a certain way in the past doesn't mean it will happen the same way in the future. Nor does it universally apply to everything in our lives. We need to be aware that we can change, that we can achieve our fullest potential and have the life we've always wanted. We just have to change our beliefs."

"That sounds easier said than done. How are we supposed to change our beliefs?" Eve asked in bewilderment, staring challengingly at Grace.

"Changes come from accepting that many of the influences from the past are not based in reality; rather, they are an illusion, which we continue to perpetuate with our thoughts. We need to believe that we can dissolve our limiting beliefs just by becoming aware that they exist and that they have nothing at all do with us personally.

"Limiting beliefs create a mould, a fabrication, very much like creating a pâpier mâché ball from newspaper and a balloon." Grace dug up a smooth, round stone that was half buried in the sand. From behind her, she picked several leaves off a low-growing shrub. "Labels and judgments, experiences and impressions accumulate over time. Layer by layer, we take these truths and plaster them over the top of our true potential, just like gluing layers of newspaper strips around the balloon, until it forms a mould, or a shell—the ego, or burden body, or shadow self," Grace explained as she wrapped leaf after leaf around the stone until it was completely covered with several layers. "However, this shell is not a genuine reflection of who we are. In fact, we're still in there, just like the balloon or stone. Inside, we are perfect and whole, but on the outside we have a big, bulky façade, or sham, as our identity."

Eve shook her head. "And to think I've carried that weight around with me all these years."

Grace let the leaves unravel, falling silently to the sand. "If we realize that all of the hurtful and negative ideas that we have about ourselves are completely false, then we can enter into the present moment with a new sense of who we *truly* are and what our *actual* potential is. It is very liberating." She handed Eve the stone. "This is how we start to climb out of our ruts.

"Limiting beliefs are not only the cause of our ruts; they help us dig those holes even deeper. They are the repetitive, reactive thoughts and behaviours that keep us firmly entrenched in our karmic cycles. But the fantastic, empowering news is that *every one of our limiting beliefs is entirely false!*

"Remember earlier when you wondered how we change our beliefs? Well, all change begins with awareness. Once we are aware that the real us is underneath, that we have limiting beliefs that are false, not true, a complete fabrication, a pâpier mâché shell based on outdated, inaccurate information, then that enlightenment leads to a change in our perception.

We can see we are so much more than our *perceived* limitations, which leads us to a choice.

"We simply make the choice to remember who we really are—an incredible, limitless, boundless soul—and choose to believe in ourselves, to embody our fullest potential and climb out of our rut!"

Eve turned the rock over in her hand, admiring its smooth surface. "I love the simplicity of it all, to just 'make a choice'—like when you had me cross that line, making the choice between feeling good for a moment or feeling good from this moment on."

"It really *is* that simple." Grace sat up, looking at Eve. "Even when we are at the lowest point, the absolute bottom of our threshold, where we scream or cry out *'I can't do this anymore'* with all the anguish and emotion that comes of being thrust to the absolute limits of our strength and resolve, we can reclaim our sense of purpose and power by deciding that *enough is enough*. We make the unassailable, conscious choice to change our language and instead yell out with determination and will, *'I don't want to do this anymore!'* The monumental word change is going from *can't* to *don't.* That small micro adjustment in wording, however, has a profound effect on our perspective and on the ripple effect that we manifest into our experience. When we say, *'I can't,'* it implies a sense of helplessness, a feeling of being lost and uncertain of what to do and where to go. By simply restating that phrase with, *'I don't want,'* we are making a powerful choice. The decision itself is a formidable action that sets a whole chain of events into motion.

"Other than your parents and your finances, Eve, can you think of any other ruts that you have?"

"Well, I have quite a few," Eve acknowledged. "Another really big one would be how upset and lonely I get when Tom has to travel due to his job. I have a really hard time coming to grips with it. I don't know why, but whenever he tells me that he has to go away again, it sends me on a spiral of emotions, none of which are pleasant."

"So at some point he tells you that he has to travel again. You get upset, and perhaps stressed, maybe angry or frustrated. What happens when he is actually gone? How well do you cope when he isn't there?"

"Badly," Eve stated simply. "Really, it's not a good scene. I am short-tempered with the kids; I don't mean to be, but I can't seem to help it. I'm angry and frustrated, and I really don't like how I feel or how I act, but it's almost as if it's uncontrollable. I feel lousy and miserable."

"Do you ever get to the point where you think you just can't take the pressure anymore?" Grace inquired.

"Sometimes," Eve replied honestly. "Like when Tom's been gone for a couple of weeks and there's still another week to go. During those times, I feel like I can't take it anymore. I am so wound up, I could cry at any moment."

"You seem fine talking about it now. Obviously, you are not still at that breaking point," Grace observed.

"No, I'm fine now. It's very difficult, but eventually I pick myself up and carry on. By the time he gets back, I am much better."

"How do you get yourself out of that funk? You were obviously feeling very bad, but at some point something happened, something changed, and you marched onward and upward. What do you think caused the shift?"

"Well, I certainly didn't want to stay miserable forever. It wasn't healthy for me or the kids. Then with Tom back home, safe and sound, everything just gets easier."

"So essentially," Grace deduced, "you made the choice that *enough was enough*, that you *didn't want* to stay miserable. You recognized it wasn't healthy or particularly enjoyable, so you made the decision to pick yourself up out of your rut by saying, 'I *don't want* to do it anymore!'"

Eve paused to contemplate the circuitous nature of that last exchange and then smiled as she caught the implication. "Yes, I guess I changed my thought process by changing my wording from 'I *can't* do this any more' to 'I *don't* want to do this any more.' Very cool." She admired the simplicity and clarity of it all.

Grace smiled. "Exactly. Just by changing our wording, we begin to act differently because our perception about life and our situation changes.

"With the decision to *change our mind* about the situation—and really, at that point in the process, that's all that's actually happened—we are still knee-deep in the murk of our situation, but with the decision that we *don't* want to be there anymore, we take a great leap toward getting out of our rut. Just by changing our mind, our attitude, we start sending the universe a very powerful message that from this point on, things are going to be different. And they are, because we even begin to act differently. Perhaps with that decision we tell ourselves to go do something we enjoy! Maybe for you, Eve, you might start to draw. Others may listen to fun, energetic music; some may go shopping, or go for a walk, maybe putter in their gardens. The point is, up to that actual decision when we tell ourselves that we *don't* want to do this anymore, we are typically so busy wallowing in our stories and misery that we don't take the time we need for ourselves, which just keeps us stagnant and fixed in our ruts. When we decide we *don't* want to be in our ruts anymore, we start making small changes and *choices* that continue to help improve our mood and our sense of well-being; they help us feel good until, eventually, we climb right up and out of our ruts.

"There are a lot more guidelines I can give you to help you out with that process if you'd like to hear them."

"Of course I'd like to hear them." Eve laughed. "Don't stop now!"

Grace chuckled and looked at her watch. "It's already four o'clock." She stretched languorously and stood up. "I think it's time we started to head back."

Eve looked up into the infinite blue sky, marvelling at how the time had flown by. They'd spent much of the afternoon chatting, completely oblivious to the outside world. Reluctant to break the spell, Eve sighed, but she rose, nodding her head in agreement.

Chapter 7
Waffles and Wisdom

They both stood still, looking at the almost vertical drop before them. Nodding encouragement at one another, they began the quick slip and slide to the bottom, rivers of sand streaming behind in their wake. Arriving safely at the bottom, they laughed and caught their breath. After brushing dusty plumes of sand from their clothes, Grace hooked Eve's arm in hers, and they began to walk the remainder of the trail, delving back into the forest, leaving the golden dunes behind.

"Okay, so where were we?" Grace reflected. "Oh, yes, getting out of our ruts. Once we've made that pivotal decision, changing our wording from *can't* to *don't*, we continue to make choices that reflect that sentiment and keep our momentum climbing upward. But these small choices alone are not specific to just getting out of our ruts; they constitute one of the many guiding lights that help illuminate the path to fulfillment. To get out of our ruts, we need to focus on choices and decisions that make us feel good, that empower and inspire us. We also need to make a broad stroke and apply this same concept throughout all areas of our lives. We do this by being able to recognize which decisions will lead us to growth and happiness and which decisions will hold us back."

"How do you tell the difference?" Eve asked.

"When we are faced with a situation that undermines our sense of well-being, first we have to be able to truly discern what feels *good* or *right* to us and what doesn't. Next, we need to use our free will to *choose* the *feel good* option. Here is where the Waffle Meter, an amazingly simple tool, comes into play. We use it to help us distinguish between which choices will lead toward growth, joy and the expression of our soul and which choices will continue to limit us, will continue to draw another karmic consequence into our paths down the road, or if we are smack dab in the middle of a karmic conundrum, will continue to keep us mired in our ruts.

"If we generate decisions that make us feel good, they align our reality with our soul. If we fall back to our repetitive, knee-jerk reactions, we align ourselves with the ego."

Eve thought about that a moment. "Well, how can I be sure I'm making the right decisions?"

"There is no right or wrong here. Deciding to align with what makes us feel good will result in the *consequence* of new perspectives opening up for us, bringing new opportunities for growth and happiness. Deciding to follow our old patterns will result in the *consequence* of meeting up with that same lesson again, just in a different guise and possibly, as I mentioned earlier, with even more at stake. It just means that we were not ready to complete that lesson. Never worry, though, Eve. We will always get another chance," Grace said, smiling.

"Here's a story that might help clarify what I mean. It illustrates our difficulty in listening to our soul, or higher self. A man was listening to the news on TV one day and heard about an incredible storm coming his way. All residents in the area were asked to evacuate immediately. The authorities expected that the levies would break, causing the small community to succumb to the rising, raging river waters. The man told his neighbours, who were packing up to head for higher ground, that he wasn't worried because God would save him, so he ignored the warnings and held tight. When the fierce storm hit the next day, the winds pummelled his home; the rains lashed and poured down, filling his basement with water. The authorities struggled from house to house, banging on doors to make sure everyone had left. They knocked on his door and implored him to leave, but he assured them that God would save him, and he ignored their pleas for him to leave. When the levies broke, flooding his entire house, he climbed up to the roof with a few of his most precious belongings. Shortly afterward, a helicopter hovered above him and dropped a rope to save the stranded man. Again he refused, saying that God would save him. They desperately tried to convince the man to leave his home, but he adamantly refused. By nightfall, the waters had swept him away, and he drowned. When he appeared in Heaven, he was furious! He asked God why He hadn't saved him. And God replied, exasperated, 'I sent you the news bulletin, but you didn't listen. I sent the authorities to knock on your door, and again you didn't listen.' Grace shook her hands for dramatic effect. 'I even sent you a helicopter!' God exclaimed."

Eve laughed. "I hope it doesn't take me that long to figure out what decisions are in my best interest!"

"Well," Grace mused, "if we continue to cling to our old habits, we will have a very difficult time hearing the gentle messages or nudges from our soul, or the universe or God.

"Our soul naturally wants to be happy. If we are unsure about a particular decision or direction, that uncertainty or flat-out *bad* feeling is our soul's subtle relay system, trying to gently guide us toward what will make us happy or, in that man's experience in the story, lead toward safety. We just need to learn how to listen for it, how to hear it and how to discern its messages.

"Let's say our friend calls us up and asks if we want to go out tomorrow night. If our immediate response does not resonate in an overwhelming 'Yes, I'd love to,' take pause. Imagine that our friend has been going through a really rough period in her life. We know she could really use a night out and would probably benefit greatly from a kind shoulder to lean on. However, we are exhausted because we have been up early and working late all week and are not sure whether we have the energy reserves to pick us both up, so we *waffle* ... 'Should I or shouldn't I?'

Eve interjected, "Aha! Just the fact that you used the word *should* immediately lets me know something is up!"

Grace smiled. "Exactly! The *should* or *shouldn't* in that scenario alone—remember the SoS alert?—is cause in itself to make us stop and pay attention, but so is the *feeling*—how we *feel* about the situation. In this case, we are uncertain and really would rather not go out, but we *waffle* back and forth trying to convince ourselves of what to do. The messages are already there; we just haven't figured out how to listen to them!

"We've all heard the expression 'you are not the centre of the universe.' Well, I am here to tell you that indeed you are! In fact, taking care of yourself and your needs has to come first! Perhaps you've heard the saying, 'If mama ain't happy, nobody's happy.' That expression applies equally to papa, as well!" Grace said with a wink. "You see, as we move toward finding happiness, we naturally become more self-centred. We truly have to put our well-being first. As in the scenario about our friend, and many others in our lives, we are willing to bend over backward for them, even when we are fully aware that doing so is not in *our* best interest. We know that going out and staying out late will only add to our exhaustion and the depletion of our precious energy reserves, but we will do it anyway. There can be lots of reasons why we put ourselves last. It may be our limiting beliefs; our negative self-talk rearing its untimely, nasty head; not wanting to let others down; or our dislike of conflict, which we avoid at all costs. There are a multitude of reasons, but the point is, rather than being true to what our *gut* is telling us, we take that nagging feeling of discomfort and tuck it quietly away. In the case of our friend here, we really don't want to go out but end up going out anyway, *against our better judgment*, putting ourselves and our needs last, ignoring what's really in *our* best interest."

"It sounds like you're talking about me," Eve said. "I can't tell you how many times I've done things I haven't really wanted to do, and in the end, I've often regretted my decision."

"Not listening to ourselves results in a *negative* experience, in the sense that we will continue to encounter situations where we will be given plenty of opportunities to listen to our higher self. But typically we don't listen. Therefore, we end up feeling not very good about the scenario. It's only *negative* if we view feeling poorly as a bad thing. It's just a lesson, neither good nor bad. If we continue to ignore the gentle urgings from our soul, then, like the man on the roof, we will only learn the lesson after the fact. Each circumstance when we ignore the opportunity to listen to ourselves results in some sort of *negative* consequence. In the scenario about our needy friend, if we, exhausted as we are, go out without our best interest at heart, we may perhaps lose something at the restaurant, or maybe the car breaks down, or perhaps the next day we fail an exam or make a major mistake in a presentation. The result may be something as simple as not having a good time because we spend the entire time berating ourselves as we envision what we truly wanted—the soft warmth of our cozy bed."

Eve carefully sidestepped a rather prickly mass of burrs. "That's another lesson I need to learn," she said, keeping a wary eye on the shrubbery encroaching upon the trail. "How to listen to my own needs and then actually follow through with them."

"We need to learn how to recognize the *good* decision and stick with it. I mentioned the waffle meter. Any time we find ourselves *waffling* between something— for example, should I or shouldn't I?—it means we are not listening to our higher self. Instead, we are trying to convince ourselves that we actually want to, or *should*—remember our tribal beliefs—do the *exact* opposite of what we *want* to do. We need to listen to what we really want to do deep down inside and stick to our guns.

"The worst-case scenario of not seeing our friend is that she is angry and doesn't talk to us for a while, in which case we can use that time to catch up on something we've been putting off." Grace held a branch out of the way for Eve to pass. "Seriously, what's the worst that can happen? Our friend never speaks to us again? Disowns us as a friend? Well, then, what kind of friend was she, anyway? Who needs a friend like that in their lives? Part of our journey here is not only determining which decisions are best for our growth and well-being but also determining what relationships inspire or empower us. If a friendship is so shallow, or so dysfunctional, that speaking our mind or heart could be a threat to its existence, then perhaps we need to use the alignment system to help us determine whether this relationship is indeed beneficial to our health and happiness. If it doesn't *feel good* any more, pay attention to that warning; take notice of that signal. Apply the waffle meter to all areas of our lives!"

"All right, I'm game. How do I do that?"

"Well, use the waffle meter *any* time you are uncertain about something. The rule is, if we are waffling, we are not listening. It's that simple! If we want to do something, it needs to be a resounding, 'Yes! I really want to do that!,' or 'No! I'm not going to do that!' When we make a decision that way, with all our intentions resonating together, the experience will be an authentic one because it aligns with who we truly are; it aligns with our soul.

"Life is about being authentic—without the extraneous *negative baggage* from our burden bodies, our tribal and limiting beliefs. It's knowing how we like our eggs and not compromising! When faced with a decision that we waffle about, understand that it means we have not immediately answered yes or no but rather are trying to steer away from the mark, not honouring ourselves and our needs first. The waffle meter is a valuable tool. Using it often will steer us toward the decisions that align with our soul, leading us to our fullest potential, and our greatest expression and experience of happiness. And, if we use this knowledge, the ability to discern what feels good and what doesn't in our experience with our ruts, we will find our way out more quickly! Our ruts and that deep *gut* sense that something is *off* are all a part of the alignment system."

"You and your crazy tools." Eve shook her head, laughing. "First the SoS alert, then your magic wand, then the waffle meter and now the alignment system! So, what's this one all about?"

"The alignment system is an energetic barometer that lets us know whether we are acting in our best interests, whether we are doing things that make us happy and lead to fulfillment rather than heading toward self-sabotage. The waffle meter is an amazing alignment tool in our system toolbox, as are our ruts. In fact, the rut is one of the biggest barometers that our soul or the universe or God uses to let us know when we are out of alignment—we are off the mark! A rut is our soul's way of letting us know that we have jumped track and are heading in the wrong direction!"

"Wrong direction? What is the right direction?" Eve asked as they rounded a bend in the trail. The forest thinned around them, and they found themselves once more on the beach, the resort and cottages off in the distance. Nodding in agreement, they headed toward the resort.

"Knowing the *right* direction depends on a number of things. Does it feel good? Does it make us happy? Are we being authentic? If we answer yes to all of those questions, then we are headed in the *right* direction. If we do not feel good, or are not happy, or are listening to the tribe's expectations, then we are headed in the *wrong* direction. And again, I have to qualify this because there really is no *right* or *wrong* decision; one feels good, the other doesn't. It's up to us how we want to feel. If we find ourselves unhappy, that's fine, as we'll have another opportunity to be happy again. It's just a matter of how many times we want to go through these scenarios or how long we want to stay unhappy. The choice is always ours. This is how we find our way out of our ruts! The key to finding out if we are headed in the *right* direction is whether or not it resonates with what is truly important in our lives. The alignment system is always trying to bring our attention back to what really matters in our lives."

Grace stopped and turned toward Eve. "If you project yourself forward to near the end of your life, Eve, where do you see yourself? Are you sitting in a solitary chair surrounded by luxury homes, your life filled with material possessions and empty relationships? Or are you sitting on a porch swing beside your soul mate, surrounded by your children and grandchildren? Is it the stuff or the people that are important? Is it the quantity or the quality?" Grace's searching eyes held Eve's gaze. "You see, Eve, the answer to that question is *true wisdom*, the knowledge of what is truly important to us. Everything else is extraneous."

As Grace looked away and resumed the walk, Eve understood that she had just been handed information of such monumental significance that she could feel the importance of it hovering in the air around her. And she tucked that knowledge safely away in her heart.

"When we are stuck in our ruts," Grace continued, "it is the alignment system telling us we are no longer following what is truly important to us. We are caught up in the ego, following its acquisitions of our *false gods*, those things that we tell ourselves we *need* to be happy. Simply using the foundation of what really matters to us allows us to supersede the ego's pull and vanquish its hold over us so we can live that authentic life that really matters!

"So, Eve, when you are down at the bottom of the rut, caused by your reactions to your parents' beleaguering you about your future, are you thinking about what is really important to you? What really makes you happy? Is it your art, your family's love for each other and your love and respect for yourself? Or are you wallowing in all the things that you could have if you earned more money? Is it the status that a piece of paper might give you, or is it the *image* you would create in your parents'—your tribe's— eyes that you want? Are you trying to live up to someone else's expectations by trying to prove to yourself that you are more than what others have said you are? When we can truly see the motives for our actions, we are able to change our perspective quite quickly and pull ourselves out of our ruts by realigning with what is genuinely important in our lives. When we honour our true wisdom, all the other things that we thought were so important drop back into their rightful place, a part of the past that no longer applies to our authentic lives here in the present moment."

"I guess I really need to pay more attention to what's driving my actions and commit to making choices that truly reflect what is most important to me," Eve said. Shaking her head in disbelief, she continued, "You've certainly helped me to see how many of my decisions are influenced by everything and everyone else. You know, Grace," she confided, "trying to live up to everyone else's ideals and expectations is very stressful."

"Stress is another big flag in the alignment system, letting us know we are off track. If we examine stress, we will find it is really the physiological manifestation of fear—more specifically, the fear of what we cannot control. And like expectations, we cannot control other people, despite efforts to the contrary. And like people, there are a multitude of situations that we cannot control. Take our jobs, for example. We can put in extra hours and extra effort, we can make ourselves completely accessible and accommodating, but in the end, unforeseeable forces, such as the economy, that are beyond our control keep us in a state of anxiety and fear; at any moment, that pink slip could fall into our laps. Despite our best efforts to control our fate, there are still things we cannot control, and that uncertainty, that fear, creates deep levels of stress. If we have a heart condition, for example, there are certain things we can control, like our diets, our exercise regimes and any improvements we make in our mental or psychological well-being. But in the ebb and flow of life, our physical deaths are something we cannot control, and it is that lack of control that frightens us. It is that fear that manifests as a rapid heart rate or shallow breath or clammy hands."

"That makes total sense to me. Fear is definitely one of the things motivating me to upgrade my skills. Things are tight, and I don't want to lose what we have."

"Trying to hold on to things, to grasp, is another one of the ego's illusions. Everything is transient, and when we are unconcerned with what we have and how to hold onto it, there is very little to be concerned about. This applies to jobs, relationships, possessions, titles, status, etc. We are here on this planet to use and enjoy things for a certain period of time. We can't take things or labels with us, despite efforts to the contrary. Take the ancient Egyptians, for example. Their objects are still here, thousands of years later, for archaeologists to discover.

"Our physical time here must come to an end. Imagine a world where no one or nothing died or decayed. It would certainly be an awfully crowded and filthy place," Grace reasoned. "Death is nature's way of ensuring that life continues. Energy can neither be created nor destroyed; it just changes states. With our physical deaths, our concepts of ourselves just change. The essence of who we are is pure energy, that spark that keeps the flame of life alive and well inside us until we take our last breath. That vibrant, energizing force cannot be destroyed. It is simply no longer held in the vessel that we have come to know of as our body."

"That may be so, Grace, but death is not a topic I'm terribly comfortable with."

"Well, you are not alone. Our biggest fears center around death and dying. One of Buddhism's many gifts is to encourage us to contemplate death, to realize that physical death will come to all of us in time. We need to be motivated by life itself rather than allowing the fear of death to motivate our thoughts and actions. Fear of death drives many of us from one transient, fleeting thing—be it a job, relationship, possession—to the next, in an effort to camouflage our discomfort. If we were truly living without fear, our lives would be inspired by enjoying each and every moment with joy and gratitude. Instead of desperately trying to hold onto the moments that have passed, and scrambling to grasp at the moments yet to come, we could be enjoying ourselves right now. Think about this for a moment … if we gave up our need to *control* and *hold,* if we just let go, *what would be left to be stressful about?*"

Eve did. She considered what would happen if she didn't worry about how things worked out, if she could just let the future take care of itself and let whatever was going to happen, happen. She realized that she needed to detach from and view all her possessions—the house, the car, all the accumulated stuff that makes a house a home—as just things, as opposed to an extension of herself or who she *thought* she was. And if she removed the fear of loss, for even a moment, and along with it the need to control everything in her life, she could genuinely feel a sense of ease. She felt her entire body relax.

"The alignment system is trying to tell us that we need to align with what is important and let go of everything else. Any time we do not feel *good*—be it about a decision, a situation, a relationship, our thoughts or fears—it's the alignment system, our soul's way of trying desperately to get our attention. It's just like being sick. If we catch a cold, a runny nose, sore throat and raspy cough are all symptoms of an infection in our body. The alignment system works exactly like that, giving us the symptoms of ruts, stress or general feelings of discomfort, fear, malaise, sadness, anger, guilt, doubt, etc. to let us know we have lost touch with our true priorities—what is genuinely important to us."

As they reached the resort, Grace looked toward the tidy row of cottages that dotted the shore. "Do you need to get back for your family?" she asked.

"Oh, no. I'll be lucky if I see them before my head hits the pillow."

"Won't they be hungry for supper soon?" The smell of barbeques and charcoal permeated the air around them and filled their senses.

"They'll stop at some local diner to eat and then head right back out. Apparently, fish bite better in the evening," Eve explained. "I think the evening fishing is the crescendo of a fine day of relaxation. How about you, though, do you need to get back?" As she said it, she felt slightly apprehensive, hoping that she could keep Grace to herself for just a little bit longer.

"No, I think our husbands went to the same fishing academy. They'll be back after dusk, usually when the mosquitoes start biting more often than the fish," she said with a laugh. "Are you hungry? They do make a lovely dinner here." She motioned to the resort's only restaurant, the Boathouse.

Before her stomach decided to register its opinion on the subject, Eve happily agreed. "I think that would be a great idea!"

They stopped at the deck where Grace had left her bag earlier that morning, and, miraculously, it was still right where she had left it. Eve looked out at the beach. The shadows were longer, and the teeming mass of bodies had gradually slipped away. There were still plenty of families gearing up for barbeques while their kids splashed in the water, but the atmosphere had become more festive with the anticipation of spending the evening together, talking and reminiscing over food and drinks.

Chapter 8

It's All Good

They made their way up to the restaurant. Every Saturday night, the small, family-oriented establishment went all out for their clients, serving a large buffet of everything under the sun, especially locally caught fish. The hostess seated them at a small booth near a window, away from the general ruckus of the room.

"Can I get you anything to drink?" she asked.

"I would love an iced tea," Eve said, and looked over at Grace.

"Make that two." Grace added, "And can we please have two glasses of water—mine with no ice, a lemon and a straw."

Eve laughed. "I'll take her ice, and I'll have mine with a lemon and a straw also."

"No problem," she assured them. "You're welcome to try the buffet or to order from the menu. Your waitress will be with you shortly," she said, placing menus in front of them.

After browsing the menu, they decided to walk over and check out the buffet. There was such a large assortment of tantalizing dishes to choose from that they decided to forgo the menu, and they filled their plates.

Once seated at their table, Eve looked down. "Oh, my, I think my eyes might be a bit bigger than my belly. I'm not sure I can eat all this, but it looks so good." She had mounded her plate full of pasta, roasted vegetables and garlic shrimp, and added a generous helping of her favourite, Caesar salad, for good measure. The smell of garlic from the salad and shrimp made her mouth water in anticipation.

Grace had filled her plate with an assortment of salads and cheeses and a thick slice of freshly baked bread. "These salads look delicious. I'm looking forward to trying the arugula salad with pine nuts and cranberries—such an interesting combination," she said, taking a bite.

The waitress approached their table. "Is everything to your liking?"

"Everything tastes absolutely wonderful, thank you," Eve replied, as Grace nodded in agreement.

While they ate in companionable silence, Eve took a few moments, trying to digest their conversation thus far. It seemed incredibly simple. If you are feeling miserable, you've lost track of what is important to you. When she was younger, there was a real push to keep up appearances, to keep up with the Joneses. She thought that this *need* had mellowed over the years. But she considered her family's financial situation—if she were completely honest with herself, it wasn't just fear that was propelling her to go back to school to upgrade her degree. It was her misguided *compulsion* to stay ahead, or to just stay even with everyone else around her, which always pulled her back into a state of melancholy. She wanted desperately to overcome that pressure to fit in, to be accepted; she knew that, in the end, it really didn't matter because status wasn't what was truly important to her. Grace had helped her to realize that. *But how do I kick those annoying habits for good?* She knew it was a habit, this knee-jerk behaviour that pulled her into a rut just because she wanted all the things everyone else had. If it was just a matter of remembering what was important, and to her, that was certainly her family. Really, if she broke it down even further, it was the love they shared that really mattered. And she knew they could have that anywhere. Honestly, it didn't matter if they lived in a smaller house or had less stuff, pomp and circumstance. Eve sighed. *Introspection is a lot of work*.

"I'm just going to powder my nose," Grace said and smiled as she excused herself from the table.

For a brief moment, Eve just stared at the empty seat, but then she turned and gazed absently out the window, twirling her pasta aimlessly around her fork. She tried to think of all her biggest ruts. Finances were definitely one of them. Her husband's travelling was certainly another. When they were married, she told him up front that domestication was not her strong suit and that they needed to enter into this commitment as partners, which he readily did. Tom took care of the laundry; he helped get the kids off to school; he was a loving husband and wonderful father. That made his absence even more painful when he went away. She had stayed at home to raise the kids, a decision they both agreed to willingly, but seeing him travel to distant places and experience new adventures left her feeling slightly bereft. She wasn't jealous of his success, nor was she resentful in any way, but there was a feeling of loss that she wasn't a part of it. It was also very difficult to manage the kids on her own when she relied so much on his help. It's not that she couldn't do it—of course she could. Like everyone else, she knew she had the inner reserves to do whatever needed to be done whenever life pushed her to her limits, but she didn't want to have to. And as she told Grace earlier, she didn't like how it made her feel. That was definitely becoming a theme she recognized; being in a rut didn't feel good!

It was all coming together! *Now I get it!* She grinned, remembering what Grace had said about the alignment system. *When I'm not feeling good it's a symptom, a reminder that what I'm worrying or ruminating about is not aligned with my highest priority, the most important thing in my life.* Rather than focusing on love, happiness and what she did have, she was lamenting about what she didn't have, or what she *thought* she didn't have. She cocked her head to the side. It was as if a lightbulb had suddenly switched on in her head. She smiled excitedly. *What other ruts can I think of?* she wondered.

Her relationship with one of her co-workers was another sore spot. The woman constantly belittled her, taking the joy out of every success Eve had with incessant, negative attacks. Eve loved her job, but every time she had to work with that woman, it was as if she were walking into a vacuum of negativity, where all the positive, upbeat energy she would like to be giving to her customers was being sucked right out of her. She knew it was becoming just a matter of time; either that woman went or she went, and that really bothered her.

Then there was her relationship with her parents. She now understood that it was her own thought processes, which revolved around her unproductive, misguided feelings and emotions of guilt and fear, that were causing the strife in that relationship. In fact, if she looked at all her ruts carefully, they all boiled down to unproductive thoughts and powerful emotions. In the middle of a rut, she would be thinking very negative thoughts, and her emotions would be either at the breaking or boiling point. *Hmph!* she considered. *If I could somehow manage my emotions and control my thoughts, my life would be a lot simpler. Of course, it would be really neat to see pigs fly too.* She smirked.

Eve watched as Grace made her way back to the table. Waiting until she was seated, Eve asked, "I understand that holding onto what is important can help us out of our ruts. But how can I possibly remind myself about that when I'm stuck there, lost in the rampage of pervasive emotions and negative thoughts?"

"There's a great expression out there—fake it till you make it. And that's exactly how we remind ourselves," Grace said, biting into another piece of crusty bread slathered with butter.

"At some point, we decide that we will no longer fall prey to our ruts. At some point, we will see that hole in the sidewalk and decide we want nothing to do with it. Our ruts, however, have a power of their own and pull us in, relying on our knee-jerk, unconscious behaviours, thoughts and actions. It's almost as if that rut, that hole, calls out to us. 'Fall in,' it beckons. 'Repeat your unconscious behaviours. Come fall in again!' The rut has magnetism; we feel drawn into its haunting familiarity. And once lost in the catacombs of our agonized emotions and tormented thoughts, it takes a tremendous amount of enlightened *knowing* to break its enticing force, its siren's call. But until we *know* we can walk past that rut without falling in, we have to first *convince* ourselves."

Raising her eyebrow, Eve shot Grace a quizzical look, causing Grace to laugh.

"Let me explain. Take the example of confidence, for instance. Remember when we spoke about confidence as a limiting belief? We tend to base our decisions on whether we have succeeded or failed at something similar in the past. If we cling to that limiting belief, we will manifest that *perceived* outcome into reality. And by manifesting, I mean exactly that. In thinking that we are not very good at a particular activity, we have already resigned ourselves to the possibility of failure. Essentially, with our *assured* thinking, we create a self-fulfilling prophecy, and just as we thought we would, we most likely will fail. In contrast, if we believe we *can do* something, because we *know we can*, then we will put a lot of energy into our success and will usually succeed. Do you recall when we spoke about learning to walk? We don't even need to think about walking anymore; we're so confident in our ability, we *know* we can. We totally believe in ourselves and our abilities!

"We need to be able to differentiate between belief in confidence and *knowing* or certainty. If it is a confidence issue, we can use the waffle meter to help us determine whether or not we are allowing it to hold us back. For example, say we are applying for a job. In the interview, the manager asks us, 'What are your weaknesses?' How might our *lack* of confidence answer this question? If our *lack* of confidence could speak … what would its answer be? 'Well, I have a crooked nose, my butt is really big, I'm not actually qualified for this job, I don't know anyone here and that makes me really uncomfortable, I can't spell—thank goodness for spell check,' our *lack* of confidence would chuckle, and on and on would go the litany of negativity.

"But how might we answer that question if our *lack* of confidence was on vacation in Bermuda? 'Weaknesses? Why, I don't have any.'" Grace grinned. "Ooh, but who says that? That's not the *right* answer. Everyone is supposed to have faults and foibles. Why? Who says so? Think on that for a moment. Who determines what our weaknesses are? A child may be labelled free-spirited, curious and determined by one person but downright obstinate, nosy and stubborn, with ADD, by another. Faults, limitations and weakness are all about perspective. One person's trash is another's treasure; it's all in the eye of the beholder. Each and every one of us is looking at the world and ourselves through our own coloured sunglasses, through our own judgments and opinions. *None of us are objective.* Faults, limitations and weaknesses are just other forms of limiting beliefs. *Since all limiting beliefs are subject to perspective, they are all, by that very nature, completely false.* If we can, through awareness, change the way we view ourselves, resulting in the novel realization that all limiting beliefs are completely false, we can simply *choose to see ourselves without any!* And if we make a consistent effort to see ourselves as complete, and make the choice to believe in our abilities and our potential, eventually we will *know*, with our whole being, that we can do or be anything or anyone we want!"

Eve finished her salad, wiping her mouth on a napkin. "What a novel idea: 'one person's trash is another's treasure.' That if I choose to see myself as complete—to know that I am whole, without any weaknesses or limitations—then I am."

"Knowing transcends the ego and involves a deep, organic, unfailing understanding of ourselves and our potential. This is a knowing from our soul, our highest self. Yet, as far as karma is concerned, we are more than welcome to continue going through all of the trouble of trial and error, of building up our confidence, layer by layer, and then, when we are uncertain, letting that belief in confidence hold us back with doubt and uncertainty. However, if we sincerely want to break our karmic cycles, we can *choose* to just skip all that uncertainty nonsense and *know* we can! It's as simple as that!"

"As simple as that, eh?" Eve mulled the phrase over in her mind.

"Because the simpler things seem too easy, we say things like 'No, that can't be right,' 'That's not it,' 'We have to struggle,' 'We have to grin and bear it,' 'No pain, no gain.' Remember, there are no *rights* or *wrongs* here. We always have a choice—to choose struggle or to sidestep that whole mess and just know it will all work out. However, our logical minds tend not to like that second option, so we have to use the *fake it till you make it* approach.

"We have to *trust, to have faith* that things will work out. We have to remind ourselves of all the successes we have had in our lives, so that we can *believe* in ourselves. Then, once we have reached a certain level of confidence, we have to continually tell ourselves that we can do or be anything or anyone we want. Eventually, after enough positive pep talks, we will *know* we can. This is how we take the belief of confidence and turn it into unshakeable *knowing*; and we do it just by adjusting our thoughts.

"Just like earlier in the job interview example, we can let our confidence determine the outcome, which will be either positive or negative, depending on our experiences with job interviews in the past and, therefore, our belief about the subject. Or we can open ourselves to new possibilities, wipe the slate clean and *believe we can!* Regardless of what has happened in the past, and irrespective of our typical knee-jerk thoughts on the subject, we declare that we are perfect for the job, that we are qualified and that we are totally amazing! We *fake it till we make it!* All we are doing is replacing one belief, the concept of confidence, with another, the concept that anything is possible. Given enough time and repetition of these types of thoughts, we begin to create a powerful thought wave that will sweep us toward knowing."

"That sounds promising. Does this 'fake it till you make it' approach only work on lack of confidence?" Eve asked, sprinkling some parmesan cheese onto her pasta.

"This fundamental metamorphosis can be applied to all of our limiting beliefs, not just to areas where we lack confidence. Adopting the belief that anything is possible, that we can truly do or be anything or anyone we want, and then affirming that belief through our actions and words will have incredible repercussions in our lives. If we replace any and all negative thoughts, feelings, words and actions with their powerful antagonists—the joyful, wonderful, self-assured, worthy, loving and happily positive vibrations, thoughts, feelings, words and actions—then we will begin to see momentously positive changes, opportunities and circumstances manifest in our lives. By replacing a limiting belief with an affirmation, we *choose* to think, speak and act in a manner that will bring us happiness, fill in our ruts and stop our karmic cycles."

"You mean an affirmation can do all of that?" Eve asked surprised.

"Affirmations are incredibly powerful tools we can use to help us on our *fake it till you make it* path toward knowing. One of my personal favourites is *it's all good!* Even if we think it *isn't* 'all good,' perhaps we are just unable to determine the benefit of the lesson right at that particular moment. But if we go out on a limb and detach from our need to understand everything, we can then focus on the eventual enlightenment the lesson will bring, rather than dwelling on the obstacle itself. We can appreciate that it truly will be 'all good'; therefore, it is, by default, right now *all good!* We can grasp that concept a little easier if we consider hindsight. When we look back on a circumstance that seemed very difficult at the time once we are safely removed from the emotional upheaval of the situation, we can reflect upon it and see the silver lining in the obstacle. Despite being difficult, something positive, some good, came from the adversity. But hindsight is twenty/twenty," Grace reasoned. "The point is to realize that it will all work out *while* it is happening, *while* we are knee deep in the situation, to know that, one day, we will be able to look back and realize that somehow, something positive came from it all. In essence, it was *all good.'* The key is to just affirm it now!

"Say it at every opportunity you get, Eve. Whenever someone asks you about your life or your circumstances, declare, 'It's all good.' Even if someone says something negative, you can counteract with, 'You know what? That's okay because it's all good.' They may not get it, but you can just smile and hold firm to your *belief* that *it's all good.* Say it often! Make it your mantra, your personal motto. Then, gradually, over time, with enough repetitions, you will truly begin to believe it. 'You know what? It *is* all good!'"

Eve put down her fork and looked at Grace. "You know what? I like that. 'It's all good' will become my new favourite saying from now on."

"Great! That's when the magic starts to happen. By declaring it's all good, by faking it till we make it, we actually begin to make it all good! Our attitude gradually begins to change, without any effort on our part, and positive situations and circumstances come into our lives that reaffirm our new rosy outlook. Things really do become all good!"

"I look forward to seeing all the positive changes this will bring into my life." Eve beamed.

"Affirmations create positive images in our mind. Just by choosing certain words, we alter our thoughts, which begin to create a positive reality around us. We set up an efficacious cycle of positivism. We manifest a new reality—things in our lives actually do become good. We begin to unequivocally believe that we can do or be anything or anyone we want to be. This becomes such a powerful self-fulfilling prophecy that we will see its success and fulfillment all around us. It's only a matter of time before that belief turns into unequivocal knowing, because in the end, as it was in the beginning, it really is and was all good! *And now we really know it!*

"We all *know* how to create a bad day. If we wake up in the morning and stub our toe, we can say, 'Oh, that's how it's going to be, is it?' Then the whole mess of a day unravels, one bad experience after another. After all, we *knew* it would. So if we reverse our thoughts, focusing on thinking positively, using our thoughts, words and actions to reflect the kind of change we *wish* to see in our lives, then we create a good day instead. *What we project is what we get!*'"

"You've opened up a whole other world to me, Grace. Before today, I never realized how powerful my thoughts were."

Finishing the last remnants of salad on her plate, Grace continued. "Remember when I asked you to consider each and every thought you have as a prayer, or a personal wish, that gets sent out into the world and is always answered? If we could all rationalize and accept that concept, we would realize the importance of choosing our thoughts and words very carefully! Positivity begets positivity; negativity begets negativity. When we constantly send out the same types of signals into the world, they begin to coalesce, to join together, and with their combined weight they generate a powerful gravitational force that attracts *like to like* back into our experience. In other words, depending on what our overall focus is—whether we are feeling and thinking *positive* thoughts and emotions or whether we are focused on negative ones—we will essentially have our *sentiments*, our *prayers*, answered.

"When we repeatedly send out the same messages, our reality will reflect our attitude. If our attitude or messages are negative, that keeps our karmic cycles alive and well. And with an active karmic cycle, we will encounter plenty of obstacles and challenges in which we always have the opportunity to try, once again, to find a positive outlook. Realizing that our thoughts and words create our experience equips us with a tremendous amount of knowledge and power, because we now know that just by *changing our thoughts*, we can change the way our entire lives manifest around us. Like Mahatma Gandhi said, 'You must be the change you want to see in the world.'"

"Wow, the concept of our thoughts joining and their combined weight creating a gravitational pull, drawing whatever we think most about back into our experience, is a powerful example." Eve almost shuddered. "I can see how important it is for everyone to try and keep their thoughts positive."

"And one of the best ways to help us stay positive is to use affirmations. Affirmations are positive words, spoken in the present tense using *I*. When spoken with feeling and repeated often enough, they have the ability to affect our thoughts. They help us transcend the false perceptions of our limiting beliefs by allowing us to counteract our negativity with the concept that anything and everything is possible. They help us *fake it till we make it*! Or we can use them to counter a specific limiting belief. If, for example, our internal bullies are berating us with such demeaning comments as, 'I'm such a wimp' or 'I'm fat,' we counter with a positive affirmation such as, 'I am strong and capable' or 'I am healthy and happy.'"

"You know, I've tried affirmations in the past, but I always thought it was some sort of willpower thing; a mind-over-matter, force-my-way-through-it kind of exercise. I never even considered the concept of using them to change my thoughts." Eve shook her head in wonder.

Grace reached into her bag and pulled out a piece of paper and a pen and started writing. "Here is a list of my favourite affirmations. 'I am complete.' 'I have everything I need within me.' 'I am grateful for all that I am and for all that I have.' 'I believe in myself.' 'I have the strength to manifest my personal potential and the personal power to succeed.' 'I am confident and strong.' 'I am worthy; I matter.' 'I believe that anything is possible.' 'I create a positive, loving, healthy reality for myself.' 'I lovingly accept what is.' 'I choose growth and opportunity.' 'I engage in compassionate, loving, positive thoughts.' 'I freely give myself permission to be authentic, to truly be who I am.' 'I allow peace, joy and happiness into my life.' 'I trust and accept who and where I am.' 'I embody my fullest potential.' 'I am supported and loved.' 'I trust the wisdom and guidance of my higher self.' 'I trust and surrender to the intelligence of the universe.' 'I let go and let God.'"

She handed Eve the paper. "Pick one or several and repeat them often. Repeat them whenever you need extra strength or to reaffirm what is truly important in your life. Use them as a gentle readjustment of your thought patterns to help you create the life of fulfillment you are searching for! And remember— *it's all good*!'"

Chapter 9
Alchemy

They had just finished dinner. Eve perused the dessert menu with childlike enthusiasm. Not accustomed to eating dessert after dinner, she found herself drawn inexplicably to a photo of a luscious-looking crêpe filled with raspberries and custard, served with a scoop of vanilla ice cream. She looked up hopefully at Grace. "Are you, by any chance, getting dessert?" she asked.

Grace had, by that time, picked up her own copy of the dessert menu and was silently absorbed in its pages.

"They have a beautiful-looking crêpe on page four, the one with raspberries in it, but I can't fathom how I could fit it all in after such a big dinner," Eve lamented.

"Well, we could split it," Grace offered. "One crêpe, two plates?"

"That's a wonderful idea!" Eve agreed. She couldn't believe how happy she felt right now. Everything just seemed lighter. Even the energy, the atmosphere, of the room was jovial, and she had to admit she was having a wonderful time with Grace.

The waitress had just finished taking their dessert order when Eve, feeling a vibration against her leg, nearly jumped out of the chair. "Oh! My heart!" She reached instinctively for both her heart and her cell phone.

She looked at the number on the screen. It was her workplace calling. *Well, at least it isn't Tom or the kids—Tom only calls if it's an emergency.* She looked across at Grace. "I need to take this; it's the bookstore where I work. They don't usually call me at home and rarely, if ever, on my cell phone." Eve answered the phone. To her surprise, Kathy, one of her co-workers, was on the other end. It was a very brief phone call, and in the span of a few minutes, Eve's entire mood darkened to both frustration and anger. By the time she rang off, Eve was positively livid.

"Everything okay?" Grace asked cautiously.

Eve placed the phone on the table and shook her head in disbelief. "That was Kathy. A very inconsiderate—no, actually, a rather nasty—

person who clearly decided it was very important, somehow, to ruin my vacation."

Grace waited patiently as Eve collected her thoughts.

"You know," Eve began, "I've tolerated this woman making snide comments about me to some of the other ladies I work with. I have even tried to take the higher road and tell myself not to stoop to her level or get caught up in her twisted world. But this takes the cake!" As if on cue, the waitress placed the crêpe on the table.

Eve sighed. Peering down at the wonderfully scrumptious-looking dessert, she felt her gut heave, and she pushed the plate away. "I'm sorry, Grace, I've lost my appetite. I was feeling so light and peaceful, and well, now ..." She thought delicately about the current fire that was rising inside of her with outright indignation. "Now I'm not." *That, perhaps, is slightly understated*, she mused.

"Yes, I can see that," Grace remarked. "In fact, I'd say you look rather piqued."

Eve smirked at that. "Yes, rather piqued indeed," she answered. "Kathy has—well, in my mind—been out to make my life miserable ever since I started working at the bookstore. Well, no, that's not entirely true," she admitted reluctantly. "We actually hit it off quite well when I first started, but when the manager asked me to be a key holder two months ago, which basically just means she trusts me to lock up or open the store, Kathy didn't take the news too kindly. She was quick to point out that she had been working there for about a year and was not privy to the keychain herself. Ever since then, she has been quite vociferous to the customers and my co-workers about any flaw that I might possess and, I think, makes up a few, just for good measure. My boss hasn't really been of much help in the situation, telling me that I'm basically overreacting. But this," Eve said, motioning toward her phone, now resting benignly on the side of the table, "in my mind, this is the lowest she's sunk. She knew I was on vacation, and rather than let my boss call me or let me find out when I got back, she decided it was her duty as a 'friend' to inform me that the company has just announced that they'll be laying off some of the part-time staff—this, of course, doesn't affect her since she is full-time.

"Honestly, how does one person's greed or insecurity cause them to be so downright nasty or insensitive? I can't recall a single thing I've done to make her treat me like this. I didn't ask for the *promotion*, if that's what you want to call it. I didn't step on anyone's toes or talk behind anyone's back. Yet she's making my job a living nightmare, and that really hurts because

I love working there. I love the customers and my other co-workers. It's really a wonderful place to work, all except for this huge mess and stress caused by this one woman!" She took in a deep breath.

"I see." Grace looked across at her. "And now that you've gotten all that off your chest, how are you feeling?"

"Angry and frustrated." She looked at Grace with exacerbated bewilderment.

"So talking about it didn't help?"

"No, I suspect it made it worse! I think I'm even angrier now than I was when the call ended."

Grace replied, "Good. I'm glad that you recognize your emotional reaction." She paused to examine Eve carefully. "And what about your physical symptoms? Your face is a bit flushed from the episode. Anything else you might be feeling?"

Eve looked at Grace in disbelief. "Why?"

"Just humour me." Grace smiled charmingly.

"Okay. Physical symptoms? Well, my appetite is gone," she affirmed, as she looked across at the plate of melting ice cream with a crêpe floating in the middle. "And I suppose my stomach is actually a bit sore, or certainly tight. My hands are a bit shaky. I am extremely tense and very agitated and more than a little upset! And, upon further reflection, I feel like I'm getting a headache." She completed her mental and physical survey.

Grabbing the pen from the table where she had placed it, Grace reached into her bag for another piece of paper. "Good. Now I want you to write down exactly how you are feeling. Include all the things you left unsaid, including any choice pieces of profanity that you feel welling up inside. I don't want you to hold back anything. I want you to write down how angry you are. Pull out everything she's ever done in the past that has culminated in this moment. Get really livid, and tell the paper exactly how you feel! Don't even think of censoring yourself. I'm not going to take the letter from you. In fact, no one will ever read it. I want you to be certain of that." She looked intently at Eve. "This little note is for your eyes only. It is not meant for anyone else, so be brutally honest about your feelings and your reactions."

Eve took the proffered paper and stared blankly at it for a moment. "No one is going to read this? Ever?" she asked, just to reassure herself. "And basically, you want me to swear, moan and scream?"

"That's right, to both questions." Grace smiled.

Eve bent her head down over the paper and summoned all her burning and buried hostile energy. She began to write casually how the whole mess had started and very quickly found her writing picking up speed and intensity. Her anger spilled from the ink onto the page in big, block letters of indignation and resentment. It didn't take long before she was caught up in the emotion of injustices, past and present.

When she had used up most of the paper, Grace quietly slid another piece near her elbow. This Eve quickly employed, settling in on page number two. By the time she reached the other side, she had begun to slow down, feeling rather exhausted. She put the pen down and looked up. "I think I'm done," she stated, somewhat surprised. "What do I do with it?"

"Just fold it up and put it in your pocket for now." Grace waited until Eve had tucked the note safely away before continuing. "How do you feel now?"

"Tired."

"Are you still angry?"

"I guess so, though not nearly as much as I was earlier."

"Good! I want you to realize the difference between a *constructive* release of energy versus a *counterproductive* release of energy.

"When we are reeling from the aftereffects of having our triggers pushed, we will often call a friend or confidante and relay the injustices that have been set upon us by our current circumstances. We will moan and complain and basically work ourselves into a frenzy, whereby we relive and re-experience the emotional trauma all over again. Our wonderful, well-meaning friends will naturally take our side or agree about the poor treatment inflicted upon us, justifying our very one-sided, limited perspective on the subject. This type of process usually just reinforces our hypersensitive and over-stimulated trigger, and we aren't actually able to release any of the pent-up energy that we've been holding on to from the initial situation. We just keep working ourselves up, allowing our emotions to escalate. And, as you can see, this is rather counterproductive!

"We tell *our story*, we tell *our side*. We get caught up in a vicious cycle of reliving having our triggers getting pushed, over and over again, as we dwell on the subject. Our stress levels, including any number of physical and emotional responses, all increase. This is exactly what happened to you, Eve, when you got off the phone and proceeded to fill me in on the situation with your co-worker, Kathy. This is just one of the fascinating things about our ruts."

"Ruts!" Eve exclaimed. "I thought we settled all that. You know, 'It's all good!'"

Grace smiled. "Remember when I said that the path to getting out of our ruts is really quite simple? That we have to make the choice to leave our knee-jerk thoughts, reactions and behaviours behind us and then continue to make positive adjustments, little baby steps along the way, until we are out completely? We change our wording to, 'I *don't* want to do this anymore' and then find a powerful affirmation to repeat, repeat, repeat—we *fake it till we make it*, until we develop confidence in our new approach and outlook, until we *know* with certainty that we can overcome our challenges and obstacles, until we *know* we can succeed. At that point, we declare 'I *won't* compromise on my happiness,' and we decide that second best or picking ourselves up and dusting ourselves off are no longer acceptable. We make the powerful decision that, from that point on, we will focus all our energy and decisions on *feeling good*. For each one of our ruts, the process really is that simple, that straightforward. However, this process is much easier when our ruts are dormant."

"Dormant? How can ruts be dormant?" Eve stared wide-eyed at Grace, utterly confused.

"In other words, the reactive behaviours or thought patterns are something we know we need to work on, but we are not, at that particular moment, attaching an emotional reaction to it. It is something we can look at, calmly and rationally, as we work our way out of our ruts. For instance, if you are reflecting, Eve, on the limiting belief of being a 'wimp,' you can think of an affirmation to counteract that, such as, 'I am strong and confident.' You can *fake it till you make it*, repeating the affirmation often, allowing it to motivate you to make small changes in your life. But for some of our really persistent and pernicious ruts, like the one brought to the surface by that contentious phone call with your co-worker, Kathy, we find ourselves suddenly thrust knee-deep in the murk and mire of our unconscious, emotional reactions. Before we can use something as powerful as an affirmation, we need to do some damage control! If someone pushes one of our buttons, causing us to immediately fly off in a rage or drop into a pool of melancholy, it's going to take a little bit of effort to climb out of that particular hole, that rut, at that moment. That emotional reaction is the alignment system's way of informing us that we are falling back into a pattern of behaviour that we have been unconsciously perpetuating throughout our lives."

Eve grabbed her cell phone and stuffed it back into her pocket. "I think I'm going to need an extension ladder to pull myself up out of this rut! I can't believe how strong my emotional reaction was to her phone call." Eve could feel herself becoming agitated again.

"That's because you are in the acute phase of a rut. This is where we are wholly, emotionally invested in our reactions. We are so caught up in our story, reliving and retelling the situation that triggered our reaction in the first place that we can't even think straight! We are consumed with our emotional responses, trapped in a frenzy of anger and/or misery. In this stage, it's very difficult to manoeuvre around the turmoil long enough to think clearly about the situation at hand. We have to find a way to discharge the built-up negative emotional energy.

"During the *acute phase*, the alignment system is in overdrive, letting us know that we need to do something about the swirling menace of energy coursing through our body. It lets us know that we need to get all that negative energy out of our body, by giving us a whole host of physical and physiological symptoms. It's similar to taking our *energetic or emotional temperature*."

"Based on my emotional and physical symptoms, I'd say my energetic temperature was soaring," Eve said, poking her fork at the soggy mass that was once their dessert.

"On the bottom of the thermometer is our base line, where we feel calm and peaceful. Then as life triggers responses in us, our stress and mercury levels start to rise, and we begin to experience symptoms. We may find ourselves easily agitated, becoming rather short-tempered with the people in our lives. We may even find ourselves yelling or crying easily. Maybe we bite our nails or begin to suffer from insomnia. As we work our way up in stress or emotional or energetic levels, our symptoms may become even more acute and alarming. We may experience chest pain or even heart palpitations. There are as many symptoms as there are situations that trigger them. And physiological symptoms related to stress are a real health risk. So it is essential to recognize that when our triggers get pushed and we feel *upset or uncomfortable*, we need to do something about the trapped negative energy that's wreaking havoc in our body and mind."

"That's interesting. I remember reading a recent article on how stress can actually cause physical symptoms in the body," Eve commented.

"Yes, and it's very important to try to recognize the subtle warnings that the alignment system sends us—to recognize the yellow or amber lights, like on a traffic light—before our symptoms turn into a serious risk to our health and well-being. We often receive subtle messages that try and tell us to slow down and pay attention to how we are feeling. Those are the amber lights, but few of us know how to recognize them until those symptoms turn into big, flaming red lights that stop us in our tracks. We need to release the negative energy early in the game, before we run out of time-outs."

Eve thought about the heaviness surrounding her after Kathy's phone call. "Sounds like a good idea to me, but how are we supposed to get rid of all that negative energy?"

"Since we have discovered that trying to talk to a biased third party is rather counterproductive, we need to figure out how to release that energy in a constructive manner. That's why I asked you to write the letter, Eve. It is one of the many LIFE lines available to help us get rid of pent-up negative energy—and we know it's negative if we don't feel good. So, in your case, Eve, your body was tense, you were getting a headache, you felt agitated, and none of that eased with the re-telling of your situation with Kathy. But you did feel better after you wrote the letter, expressing what was weighing on your heart. Depending on what our symptoms are and just how lousy we are feeling, there are a number of LIFE lines we can use to help us decompress and vent in a much more effective and efficient manner."

"I'd love to know more of those life lines," Eve acknowledged. "I really don't enjoy feeling this way."

"Well, talking to a counsellor or therapist is one way of decompressing because they will not fuel our emotional tempest. It's their job to remain completely impartial. Writing a letter can also do this for us. It gives us an opportunity to vent without holding anything back in fear of censure or disapproval. Journaling is another outlet we can use, but a caution about words on the written page. Anytime we vent, whether it's in a letter or in a journal, the emotional words that we write could be very hurtful if someone else were to read them. Our intention in keeping a journal or writing a letter is never to show those words to another human being. The writing itself is a release and, therefore, a powerfully cathartic aid to us; it is not meant as a way to hurt someone else.

"Expressing our emotions doesn't have to involve words. A non-verbal activity can be a very therapeutic way of releasing built-up tension. We can take a handful of crayons, a big piece of paper and try colouring, smearing or scribbling passionately. We can even try using our nondominant hand to allow the other half of our brain to get in its two cents' worth, as well."

"Now, that method really appeals to me." Eve's eyes brightened. "I can actually imagine how slapping and throwing paint on a canvas, and then scratching and scraping at it, would help me get rid of tension."

Grace laughed. "I see how that kind of vigorous painting could be very liberating for you, Eve. For others, however, something more subdued, like meditation, relaxation and breathing exercises, are also wonderful ways of de-stressing. As are nature walks, yoga classes and Tai Chi. Or, if we really need a more physical way to cut loose, we could try running, working out at the gym, dancing or kick boxing to help shake off that excess energy. There are as many ways of decompressing and de-stressing as there are ways of working ourselves up!

"There is one more powerful LIFE line that you can try. I call it the *vortex!* In this practice, we reach out to Mother Earth and offer Her all of our negative energy and painful emotions, which She takes into Her heart and evaporates into thin air, both literally and figuratively. Mother Earth is an amazing recycler. After all, She has been turning waste products and dead, decaying matter into beneficial, organic compost for billions of years. Fire is an incredibly transformational process, and at the heart of Mother Earth is a raging furnace, where the alchemy of transmutation takes place. Since science tells us that energy can be neither created nor destroyed—it only changes form—we offer Her all our negative, pent-up energy, and She transforms it into a state that will help sustain and support life, rather than harm it."

"That sounds intriguing. I'd love for all my troubles to just evaporate into thin air," Eve said, welcoming the possibility. "How does this vortex work?"

Grace smiled warmly. "It's quite simple; all we need for this exercise is a tree. If we find ourselves unable to get hold of the real thing, we just need to visualize one. Either in your mind's eye or in the natural world, choose a tree that is healthy and strong, with branches that reach to the sky and a trunk that's thick and broad.

"Since the crêpe never quite made it into our bellies, and we happen to be in very close proximity to the real thing," Grace said as she swept her arm in front of the beautiful view through the window, "I suggest we take a little walk outside."

They both looked down at the mess on the plate in front of them. Eve smiled apologetically. "I'm sorry. I was really looking forward to having dessert. Perhaps on our way back, we could try again. I know the restaurant is open quite late," she offered hopefully.

"Oh, don't worry about the crêpe." Grace smiled. "It was very fortuitous that Kathy called when she did. Otherwise, I wouldn't have had this wonderful opportunity to show you how to deal with an emotional stress overload."

Eve didn't know just how fortuitous that particular experience was, but she was grateful that she had Grace there to help her deal with it. She wondered for a moment what would happen when the next trigger got pushed and Grace *wasn't* there. She decided that was not a particularly pleasant train of thought and resolutely pushed it from her mind. Besides, she told herself, there was always e-mail and the phone, even if she and Grace couldn't get together.

Looking over at Grace, it occurred to her that she had no idea where Grace and her family lived. Perhaps they lived close to each other. She would have to ask her. They paid for dinner and stepped out into the beautiful summer evening.

The waves lapped softly at the shore, and the sun, heavy in the sky, sent fiery rays of brilliant orange out onto the water. Eve shielded her eyes and drank in the sheer power of the sight. *Is it possible to just dissolve into flame, right here?* she wondered. *Maybe I won't need a tree after all. Maybe I can just throw all my troubles into the sun and let it burn them away.* As she was pondering this thought and feeling rather proud of the notion, she realized Grace had moved off into the shadows near the edge of the forest. She turned her back to the blazing sun and found Grace sitting in the sand, her legs and arms wrapped around a tree trunk.

"This is the perfect size." Grace smiled and stood up, brushing sand from her dress. "Your turn."

"My turn for what?" Eve asked cautiously.

"For hugging my good friend here," Grace replied simply, patting the tree trunk affectionately.

"For hugging the tree." Eve said it more as a statement than a question, but she felt disbelief settle firmly into her features as she took in the proposition.

"She won't bite," Grace offered helpfully.

"Oh, it's a she, is it?" Eve asked as she stepped forward and looked up into the branches above her.

"Here." Grace gestured to where she had just been sitting. "Have a seat and wrap your arms and legs around the trunk, and then rest your forehead against it."

Eve looked around, feeling completely absurd and self-conscious.

"No one is looking," Grace observed. "Besides, even if they were, what does it possibly matter to you? When will you ever see these people again? And if you did run into someone again, why would it matter what they thought? What matters is the experience. And I'm about to show you a powerful way to release your negative energy."

Eve sighed, rolled her eyes up to the sky and sat down in the sand. "What do I have to lose, right?"

"Just the stuff you don't want anymore," Grace added cheerfully.

Eve ignored the nagging thought that people were going to wonder what the crazy lady who was hugging a tree could possibly be thinking. She settled in around the tree and closed her eyes. The first positive thought she had was that this was actually very pleasant. The tree was still warm from the sun, and the trunk felt solid, almost self-assured, under her skin. It seemed to give off a healing, protective energy, and Eve felt immediately drawn to its presence. She wasn't sure if it was indeed a 'her,' but she could feel a unique aliveness to the tree itself. She smiled and offered her new friend a silent *thank you* for sharing this experience with her.

Grace's voice floated out from somewhere behind her. "With your eyes still shut, Eve, I want you to just focus, for a moment, on your breath. Just watch your inhale and your exhale, and begin to feel a connection with the tree. See if you can feel its internal rhythm as it takes in your carbon dioxide and releases its oxygen, which you then take in. The two of you have a symbiotic relationship. You are each giving and receiving, supporting each other in a gesture of love and compassion. As you take a moment to make that connection, see if you can visualize the tree's outstretched canopy reaching above you. See the trunk rising upward and outward as it branches off into smaller and smaller boughs, until it ends in individual twigs and leaves. Then, visualize the roots of the tree underneath you. See the main root system, branching off into smaller and smaller parts, until it ends in the tiny hairs that draw the water and nutrients from the Earth. See those roots branching out all around you, and see those roots burrowing deeper and deeper into the Earth. Hold onto the image of those roots creating a great labyrinth that tunnels deep into the Earth's centre, to its very core.

"I want you to take a moment to ask Mother Earth for Her help. I use the image of a female entity because the Earth is typically seen as a mother figure who nurtures and supports us. It is precisely those qualities that we want to engage as we seek healing. Ask Her to please receive your pain and hurt, all your anger and indignation, all your fears and worries. Ask Her to please receive all of your negative energy so She can transform and recycle its potential into a positive, life-affirming force that will benefit everyone and everything on this planet. We always ask for permission first and wait for Her to reply, which usually comes as a feeling of peace or approval or relaxation, or just simply silence. She will never reply no. She will never refuse Her children. She is here to help us on our journey; in fact, She literally supports our every step!

"Once you feel ready to go on, use the image of those industrious roots tunnelling their way deep into the Earth. I want you to visualize all of your negative energy travelling down through that root system until you reach the core, the heart of Mother Earth. In Her core is an almighty fire that will consume your pain and transform it into radiant peace. Imagine your negative energy spiralling down into the centre of the Earth, like a giant vortex, being pulled into the Earth's core and incinerated until nothing is left but the vapour of pure potential, the pure potential of peace. And then allow that vapour, that peace, to permeate every cell in your body, as it fills the air around you. Continue releasing that negative energy until you can't cry anymore, or until you feel calm and grounded. You may be there for a couple minutes or hours; all that matters is how you *feel*. Feel the negative energy release from your body and mind. Feel your entire being fill with the peace that comes naturally and effortlessly once you create the space to let it flow back in. Peace, happiness and joy are our natural states of being. We just need to remove the albatross to find that lightness once more."

Eve did exactly as Grace explained. She took all her negativity and visualized it travelling down the roots of her tree until they formed a giant spiral. She sent that toxic waste down the spiral until she saw the flames consume her anger and frustration. Then she scanned her body, looking for any other emotions she hadn't quite dealt with, and she decided to throw them all into the fire too: her frustration over finances; hardly seeing Tom anymore; the drama with her parents; the worry over her future plans—everything she could think of she sent down the vortex, along with her impassioned tears, until they reached the Earth's centre. She envisioned her emotions and tears being transformed by the fire in the Earth's belly until they evaporated into a tranquil mist. Then she visualized that mist filling the space around her until she could feel the cool, weightlessness of it against her skin. Then she imagined taking that refreshing vapour into her pores and allowing it to fill her, until it felt as if she was breathing the peace into her very being. It was now a part of her very essence. She could feel it radiating outward, very much like the relationship with the tree. Their breath was matched exquisitely, in rhythm; as she breathed out, the tree breathed in. Here, in this veil of peace and tranquility, she was not only floating in a peaceful space, she was becoming peace itself. It was truly an incredible experience. In fact, she was so engrossed in the moment that when she opened her eyes sometime later, the late evening sun was dipping closer to the horizon, a luminous red orb that sent fingers of pinks and violets across the sky, blending together like a beautiful watercolour.

Eve, slightly dazed, looked around and saw Grace sitting in the sand by the shore. She got up slowly and walked over to where Grace was sitting and noticed that she had built a small fire.

She sat down. "Thank you," Eve whispered quietly. "That was very powerful and very …"—she searched for the words—"sacred and special."

Grace smiled. "Nature has a wonderful way of cutting through the illusion of separation, the idea that there is no connection to anything at all. It effortlessly breaks apart the misconception that we little humans are all alone, floating aimlessly in the world, with no anchor to ground us. When we allow ourselves to connect to something greater than ourselves, the ego begins to lose its grasp on our perception. We begin to see and align with a very different world, one where we have a close, intertwined, interconnected relationship with everything. Nature is a selfless guide, showing us the way to peace." Grace poked the fire with a stick. "Do you still have the letter?" she asked.

Eve reached into her pocket. "Yes, it's right here."

"It's just symbolism, but you are welcome to throw the letter into the fire, to see the literal dissolution of that frustration and pain."

Eve looked at the paper carrying its secret hostility and realized she didn't feel that way anymore. She considered it for a moment and felt that burning the letter would be oddly symbolic, a pure physical gesture of letting it all go. Although after the exercise with the tree, she realized that psychologically she already had. *This is just sentiment*, she reasoned, *a nice closure.* She placed the paper near the flame so that the edge caught suddenly in a blaze of orange. She tossed it quickly into the fire, watching it curl into itself as it blackened and disintegrated in front of her eyes. It took no more than a few seconds until it was indistinguishable from the other bits of ash that lined the bottom of the small pit Grace had created in the sand.

"Why is it that it took that kind of effort to release all that emotion?" Eve wondered aloud. "I'm not very good at expressing my emotions; I do tend to hold things in," she explained. "I think, deep down inside, I view crying as a sign of weakness. I certainly wouldn't cry in front of another person if I could help it. I guess that's probably not a good thing?"

"It's not that it's a *good* or a *bad* thing. We all have coping mechanisms—things we have done in the past that we felt we needed to do, to get us through some of the harder times in our lives, like suppressing how we really feel because we were not in a position to cope with or confront those emotions. Tactics like these become part of our survival guides, those walls we hide behind, defences that we have relied upon time and time again. And while we felt they were necessary at the time, at some point in our lives those defences may be harming us more than they are helping us. If we constantly push things away, or hold them in and tamp them down because we are afraid to deal with them or let them out, then all that negative energy and emotion gets trapped in our body, in our tissues and cells. For example, if we are carrying the weight of the world around on our shoulders, we might find it manifesting as chronically tight shoulders and neck pain."

"I guess holding in my emotions has always been one of my defence mechanisms," Eve reasoned. "And when I hold things in, it often manifests as a knot in my stomach, along with chronically tight shoulders. I'd love to get rid of all that tension."

"To release that trapped emotional energy, we need to be patient and compassionate with ourselves. Emotions can be very powerful, and confronting and releasing them can be quite scary and intimidating, akin to opening that proverbial Pandora's box. When a strong emotion comes to the surface of our awareness, we need to find whichever LIFE line works best for us and focus on our hearts while we try to breathe through the pain. Our hearts are often seen as the emotional centre of our body, and if we hold our attention there and focus on our breath, we will be able to move through the pain and truly release it. Find a slow, steady rhythm to the breath and focus on exhaling all the old, unwanted negative thoughts, energy and emotions, and inhaling all the new, peaceful, calm, compassionate positive thoughts, energy and emotions." From a small pile beside her, Grace placed the last big piece of driftwood onto the fire.

"Taking down your walls, your defences, Eve, is a slow and considerate business. You need to remove one brick at a time, focusing on only what you can handle. Don't rush to try and confront every negative memory, image, thought and emotion all in one go. Take your time. Work on them one by one, until your entire body and mind are lighter. But as each emotion or image comes into your awareness, you can't just toss it away without acknowledging it first—you have to really and truly feel it.

"The vortex and other LIFE lines are not about taking our emotions and just flushing them down the toilet. We have to really pay attention to them—we have to experience them first.

"Before we release our negative emotions and energy, we must make sure we have given our body a chance to have its say, to let us know that something is not right in our world. Then we have to convince our body that its sentiments have value and that they have truly been heard. We must invite our body, with its myriad of emotions, into the same space as our processing mind and our compassionate, loving, accepting soul. The three of us have to have a wee sit down together and agree to be in the same space at the same time. This is very similar to how the Round Table was used in Camelot. All three parties—our body, mind and soul—must listen to one another in an act of equality."

"Mind, body and soul—we always think of them individually, like me, myself and I." Eve mulled the concept over, watching as the hazy smoke drifted upward into the sky. "I've never really considered them separately—but neither have I imagined them as one, now that you mention it. That's an interesting paradox."

"Actually, they are both, in that they work together as one, but with each part having its own unique function. Our body, with its beautifully orchestrated, sensitive nervous system and its formidable survival instincts, lets us know that something is wrong by sending us negative emotions and stress. As a result of our thoughts, actions or current situation, our body sends us plenty of signals, informing us that there is danger here. Our body is constantly reacting to our external environment and to the signals our soul and mind are sending us. It's like finding ourselves suddenly face-to-face with a Siberian tiger in some dark alley. Our fight or flight system sounds the alarm and does everything in its power to try to convince us to run. But, as our mind knows, there are some situations in our lives that we cannot run away from. Perhaps it's work, a relationship or a home situation where we find ourselves unhappy but feel we are not in a position to immediately change our current circumstances. We can, using our mind, decide to make small changes to both our thoughts and actions as we *advance* toward our preferred outcome. But our mind can't overrule our body, which at that exact moment is causing stress and unease, letting us know that something in our current situation is threatening. And, the body adds, it's not particularly happy with that scenario. It just wants to get away from the tiger—or the job or the uncomfortable situation—as quickly as possible and gives us plenty of symptoms to let us know that."

"I've had plenty of tigers lurking around in my life," Eve said, laughing tentatively. She looked back at the outline of trees behind her; as if anticipating that one of those tigers would suddenly leap out from the shadows. "But most of the time I override my body's reactions. Sometimes it's just easier to ignore them."

"Ignoring things doesn't work. It's like putting a Band-Aid on a broken leg. It's like when our mind tries to use logic and reason to assess the situation and then tells our body to stop worrying about the big, scary tiger, asserting that everything will be okay. It lists the affirmations it will use and the logical outcome that will manifest just by changing our thoughts about the particular situation. Our mind may agree with our body, affirming that it too is unhappy with our current situation, but it will try to reason with our emotional body by pointing out that since we are unable to change our current situation, we need to change our thoughts about the matter and try to make the best of it. These are wonderful sentiments, but if we are just sweeping our discomfort, our emotions, under the rug, our efforts to change our circumstances will not be successful. If we decide that we are far too busy to deal with the *silly* emotions vying for our attention, we will put them *out of our mind* because our logical, rationale mind is completely *uncomfortable* with the assault of emotions brought about by our body. Therefore, we try to talk or reason our way out of our discomfort. Basically, our mind tells our body that the tiger has probably already eaten, so it's not hungry and poses no immediate threat to us. However, our body, not so easily dismissed, still sees the tiger, the threat—the job or other discomfort. It is not impressed by the mind's rationale or reasoning. Eventually, our body will become fed up with our mind's relentless rejection of its case and will have a temper tantrum—and a whole host of physiological symptoms will ensue."

"Okay, you mentioned that the mind tries to use reason to talk its way out of situations, but what happens when you ignore the threat completely?"

"Well, unless our body feels as though its concerns have been listened to, it will continue to increase our awareness of discomfort and stress by upping the ante on our symptoms and emotional or energetic temperature. Our affirmations and sincere desire to change our thoughts and behaviours will get muddled, since our body and mind are sending mixed signals into our environment. Our mind, convinced of the power of *unquestionable* logic, is trying desperately to make changes in our life by agreeing to change our thoughts. But our body is still sending out signals of discomfort, which our mind is working very hard to ignore. The signals, or vibrations, we are sending into the world are creating a neutral charge. Our mind is sending positive vibes; our body is sending negative ones. When the two waves meet, they cancel each other out, and we just keep getting more of what we had before—more tigers."

"More tigers? Pretty soon there will be an entire circus, and a monkey and a weasel to boot, all running around that Round Table of yours." Eve sighed. "I really don't need any more tigers in my life!"

Grace stirred the embers with her stick, sending a bevy of hot orange ashes into the air. "Our body and emotions simply want to be heard. But we can't try to release the emotions too quickly, without acknowledging why we are feeling them in the first place. In order to placate and release our tigers, we need to discern why they are presenting themselves in our lives. What situation has caused their appearance in our awareness? What is the exact nature of the emotions? What, specifically, are we feeling? Are we angry, upset, frustrated, hurt or dejected? Do we feel lonely, unloved, unworthy, guilty or miserable? If we are unhappy about a situation, for example, we need to say something like, 'I know I am not happy about __,' or 'I am really hurt by what she or he said about me,' or 'I realize that I have been overlooked for a raise for several years now and that makes me feel angry and unappreciated.' We need to create this kind of dialogue within ourselves every time we are in a position in which we are unhappy or uncomfortable. Then, once we discern exactly what we are feeling and why, we need to decide on the best possible strategy to find our way back to equanimity and peace."

"And I thought talking to oneself was a sign of insanity!" Eve sniggered. "However, I can see how actually having conversations with my body would be very beneficial. By holding things in, I don't usually give myself the time I need to truly confront what is bothering me, and if I do acknowledge the problem, I sweep the discomfort under the rug. It's almost as if I deny how much things really bother or upset me. Like I'm some sort of robot or superhuman who can just keep taking the knocks. But I can't. They do hurt. And I don't want to keep locking things away anymore. I don't want to keep hiding my emotions. But I must admit, Grace, this is a really alien concept for me—the idea that all three of my faculties have a say and that each one's opinion or perspective is just as important as the other."

"Alien, perhaps, but certainly worthwhile. Our soul, which is always trying to encourage and guide us on our journey toward living in fulfillment every day, tries desperately to get our mind and our body to listen to one another, since each has valid points. If all parties agree that we are not happy, that something needs to be done to find our way back to the path to fulfillment, then we need to work together to come up with a solution. Together, the three of us—mind, body and soul—must figure out how to back safely away from the tiger in our lives. We do this by acknowledging our discomfort and agreeing on a course of action. We, all three of us, acknowledge that we are not happy with the fact that we find ourselves face to face with a tiger. We listen patiently to the body's reactions by truly *feeling* our emotions—by finding a way to put into words our feelings and the situations that elicit them. Give them a voice! Let them be heard!"

"Let them be heard?" Eve asked. "Like when I spoke to you about Kathy?"

"No, this is not about describing or expressing our emotions to others but rather explaining and accepting them ourselves. Once we understand and feel our emotions, we allow our mind, through its superior ability, to deduce and reason, to suggest different solutions, different courses of action that we can follow. Then, all three of us weigh the pros and the cons, choose the best action presented, and take those steps toward happiness and fulfillment. We are, finally, all in agreement! This process allows the three of us to feel as if we have been truly heard, that all parties have had a say in choosing the best course of action, with all perspectives being addressed and considered."

"How very democratic of us!" Eve commented. "You make everything sound so easy."

"It is easy, but we have to be mindful, patient and compassionate with ourselves during this process. We *must* acknowledge the negative emotions and pain *first* and *then* release them. Send them down the vortex, send them into the wind with each breath during our walk or run, release them by setting them down on paper—write, draw or paint away our negativity—until we feel a sense of peace envelop us. Then when we apply such tools as affirmations, they will become a powerful, energy force of change, since we are all—body, mind and soul—in *energetic and vibrational* alignment. And with that kind of force behind us, we will soar to the top of the mountain, where we will truly experience a life of happiness and fulfillment," Grace asserted.

"My best friend practises yoga, and I've heard her say that our body, mind and soul must join together in union. I think I'm finally getting it!" Eve observed.

"I'm glad," Grace said and smiled. "We need to recognize that each part of us is just as important as the other, that it takes all three to navigate our experiences here in this physical world. Our body informs us about our internal and external environment, and our mind then makes a plethora of judgments, conclusions and opinions based on that information. Our soul is always trying to mediate between the two, while steering us toward happiness, peace, joy and fulfillment. It's not always an easy job," Grace pointed out.

"No, I imagine not." Eve experienced a sudden image of her kids fighting for what they wanted, each believing he was right, and her having to step in as a referee. "No, definitely not an easy job," she had to agree.

Chapter 10

Realization

The sun had set. There was only a soft glow on the horizon to attest to the fact that it had ever been there at all. Eve shivered, looking at the dwindling fire. "We need more firewood. It's much cooler now that the sun has gone down," she said, and she grabbed an island blue hoodie from her beach bag, put it on and zipped it up to her chin.

"I agree." Grace wrapped her bare shoulders in a soft, white cotton shawl and stood up. "There's lots of driftwood strewn along the beach that we can collect."

They wandered off in opposite directions, filling their arms with bits and pieces of wood, depositing them in a small pile. Grace arranged the biggest pieces in a tripod, which quickly caught, sending hungry flames licking upward into the night sky. Reaching into her bag, Grace pulled out a blue and green tartan blanket, which she spread out beside the campfire.

"Wow, what else do you have in that bag?" Eve said, and they both laughed.

"You know the Girl Guide motto—be prepared!" Grace winked.

They sat down on the blanket, wrapping the corners around their legs. Eve looked up into the moonless sky. The stars, pinpricks of silvery light, were just beginning to wake from their daytime slumber. She sighed in contentment, enjoying the serenity of the moment—the crackle of the fire, the musky smell of burning wood and, most of all, Grace's sublime company.

"Remember when we were speaking about the body, mind and soul—getting the three of them together? Well, it may not be the easiest job, but it is extremely rewarding," Grace observed as she rearranged one of the logs that had fallen. "The more our soul can get our mind to see its point of view, the more our mind becomes a powerful advocate for change. Until then, though, our mind is a minion of the ego, stuck in the unconscious, knee-jerk reactions, opinions, behaviours and judgments of our past experiences.

"Our mind is like Darth Vader in the *Star Wars Movies* when it is controlled by the ego—or the dark side. We are stuck in our repetitive, reactive thoughts and behaviours, unaware of our patterns. Essentially, we are unconscious or asleep. On a daily basis, we walk around the world like zombies, unable to break out of our ruts, following the same patterns and reliving the same circumstances. We remain stuck in the same types of relationships, with the same types of people, encountering the same types of obstacles in the same types of environments. And we are not truly happy. Then Luke Skywalker comes along in Return of the Jedi, and *feels* the good in Darth Vader and, through Luke's decision not to fight, not to *struggle* against the dark side, Darth Vader realizes the *good* inside of himself. Our mind, when it stops struggling against life and lets go of its need to control, finds calm and peace. When that happens, our soul can have an open dialogue with our mind, rather than just relying on messages sent through the alignment system. We start to wake up. We start playing our own unique roles in this life experience, rather than just role-playing the expectations of others. We find our authentic self, and life becomes empowering, engaging, fun and fulfilling. We become truly happy."

"I guess I'm not being terribly authentic," Eve said, staring into the fire. "At least when it comes to dealing with my parents, or Kathy. I mean, the situation makes me miserable, but I'm not really confronting the issues, am I? And because of that, I'm reliving the same type of situations in my life—they both belittle me, my parents to my face, Kathy behind my back. It's like you're saying—I'm playing a role, just trying to live up to everyone's expectations. I may have gone over to the dark side, Grace." She winked. "Though, I can see how, by not standing up for myself, by just letting them affect me the way they do, I keep acting like a zombie. I think I need to wake up."

"That's quite a revelation, Eve. We all need to wake up. And helping our mind on its journey from asleep to awake is the powerful practice of meditation. When our mind is truly calm and peaceful, our soul can openly communicate its desires and insight. All we need for meditation is intention. If our intention is just to be with ourselves—to discover whatever comes to the surface and to find peace and joy throughout—then any activity can be meditation. Formally, a meditation practice involves sitting in a comfortable position with the spine straight. We can use a chair or lean against the wall or sit on a pillow or cushion—whatever is most comfortable. However, we can just as easily meditate while lying down or while sipping a cup of tea in the garden or while running, dancing or walking. What changes other activities, such as running, dancing or walking, from a physical exercise into meditation-in-motion, is our intention. We set our intention to focus on just being with ourselves, with all our idiosyncrasies, all our doubts and fears, all our dreams and desires—all the parts of us. We allow each and every thought, image and sensation to rise to the surface of our awareness *without judgment or criticism.* We just notice them. We just observe ourselves. As James Cameron so eloquently pointed out in *Avatar,* we just have to 'see' ourselves. No judging, no criticizing, no negative emotional self-talk whatsoever. We accept all of us because each part has made us who we are and has brought us to this point; we wouldn't be here, reading these words, experiencing this moment, without all that has come before to lead us to now. So we honour our rites of passage, and we accept ourselves for who we really are—*a beautiful soul on a phenomenal journey.*"

Eve tossed a couple small pieces of wood onto the fire. "I remember when I was in high school, which was probably the last time I truly painted just for the joy of it. I was always painting. I had set up a small corner of my bedroom as my studio, and I would retreat away from the world and find release and solace in my canvas. I would lose myself in my art. Now when I'm gardening, I have wonderful moments of what you might call meditation, but I'm not sure how I would find that peacefulness again just by sitting."

"The only difference between painting or gardening and sitting is what you are focused on—and your intention. If your intention is to just sit with yourself, to just be in the moment, then you only need to figure out something other than your art or garden to focus on. Many meditation practices use the breath as a means of developing focus. The breath is always there, so we can follow the breath as a method to give our mind something to do instead of thinking incessantly. And one way to focus on the breath is to count. We always keep the breath comfortable and relaxed, no matter which counting practice we decide upon. For this first counting practice, we count slowly and continuously backward from thirty-nine to zero. Once we reach zero, we start all over again at thirty-nine. If we start thinking and lose our place or forget what number we are at, we simply start all over again at thirty-nine. Conversely, another exercise is to count one breath at a time. One inhale, one exhale, two inhales, two exhales, working our way up to ten inhales, ten exhales, at which point we start all over again at one inhale, one exhale. If we lose our place and or forget what number we are at because we have drifted off into thinking again, we finish with that thought and start counting all over again, beginning at one inhale, one exhale. There is no right or wrong.

"Some days we may only make it to five inhales and five exhales before we drift into thinking and have to start all over again; on a different day, perhaps we get all the way up to two sets of ten inhales and ten exhales before we lose our place. It's important, Eve, not to judge by time or duration. Don't judge any part of the practice or yourself at all! Just enjoy the process. When thoughts come into your awareness, notice them, listen to them and sort them out by whatever means your mind feels is necessary. If the thought or conundrum that floats to the surface of your consciousness is a significant one, it may take a bit of thinking to find a solution, but that's fine.

"The idea is to remain calm and rational without bringing judgment or emotion into the thought process—as if we are observing and studying the situation as a third party, as someone detached, not actually involved. This allows us to move through a stressful situation in our mind without the emotional charge associated with it. If emotions do arise, that's fine, too. Feel them, give them a voice. Let them have their say. Let our body communicate its observations and its desires. Then, when we feel we have addressed that particular emotion or thought and are ready to move on, we find the breath once more and continue counting."

"I imagine if I just sat there, my body and my mind would have an awful lot to say." Eve shook her head doubtfully. "I may not even make it past one."

"That's okay. Sitting down and getting to one is better than not sitting down at all. Don't get caught up with what you think it's supposed to look like; don't put expectations onto it. Meditation is all about intention and simply showing up. Perhaps you will find that, over time, as your commitment to your meditation practice deepens, the barrage of thoughts begins to slow down. Be patient and accepting. Let whatever happens, happen.

"As we continue our practice, focusing on our breath and counting, we may notice fewer and fewer interruptions. We may even get to the point where we feel we are *on a roll,* and for several days the thoughts do seem to slow down, thus allowing us to experience moments of *calm being,* or *quietude,* in our meditation. When we think we have this whole quietude thing all figured out, however, we may have an especially stressful day. When we sit to meditate, we find our mind on a rampage, full of thoughts, images, associations, judgments, impressions and conclusions. That's wonderful! Sort it all out and come back to the breath. Since there is no right or wrong, some days we will be able to sort through our thoughts by solving some problems or making some decisions. On other days when our mind just keeps looping and processing information and we can't find even a small semblance of calm, that's fine, too. Smile, get up and carry on with the day. See what happens tomorrow when we come back to our meditation practice. It's important to realize that meditation is a practice. It is something we decide to do with frequency. Ideally, early morning or later in the evening is best, but any time that feels good to us is a good time to find calm. For example, if we are having a particularly stressful day and wish we could just *step out of it* for a moment, then that's the perfect time to find a quiet corner and just follow our breath. We don't even need to close our eyes; however, we will find a quieter sense of ourselves if we do.

"Remember, Eve, when I had you close your eyes and plug your ears how your attention was drawn inward by turning off your busiest senses? Whether we choose to close our eyes or not, we will find quietude and calm if we can just *take five* out of a stressful day and find our breath."

Eve cocked her head to the side. "Well, now that you've explained it that way, it seems easy enough," she admitted. "My mind can go off on its rampages and ramblings, but as long as I just establish my intention to sit in the middle of it all, despite all the interruptions, I am actually meditating." She smiled. "I think I'd like to try that."

"Excellent. Here's a meditation challenge you can try, Eve. Give yourself forty days to establish a meditation practice. Find a convenient time and comfortable place where every day for forty days you can meditate without interruption. If, however, you miss a day, you have to start all over again at day one. Once you make it all the way to forty days, celebrate! But don't stop. Make meditation a daily part of your life. Like I mentioned earlier, it is truly one of the greatest gifts I can give you, Eve, and is, in turn, one of the greatest gifts you can give yourself. It will help calm and soothe your mind, it will give your body a venue to bring its needs to the table, and it will allow your soul a direct line of communication with both. On the path to fulfillment, it's a giant leap forward!"

"A time when I won't be interrupted? Hmm ..." Eve wondered how she could possibly find that. "Perhaps when I lock myself in the bathroom," she replied, laughing, knowing that even then, the kids would be knocking at the door, wondering what Mommy was doing. It wasn't just a joke, though. With a young family, it wasn't easy to find alone time.

She could possibly carve a few minutes before bed or perhaps before she woke everyone up for school. "How much time would I need?"

"One minute, five minutes, twenty minutes ... the time is not important. It's the intention that counts. Just give yourself a *moment* to discover the thoughts that come up, and just breathe through it all. If you have one minute, fantastic—that's more time than you gave yourself the day before. Relish that minute to yourself, savour it. If you can find an extra minute another day, relish that too." Grace smiled. "There is a lovely expression—the past is history, the future's a mystery, and the present is a gift, which is why we call it the *present*. So the more often you can gift yourself your 'present' moments, the longer and more frequent you'll want those moments to be. For example, perhaps you decide to practise your meditation one day while you create your art, Eve. You sneak away into your bedroom, just like you did when you were younger, armed with a sketch pad, pen and pencil, and you set your intention to just be with yourself while you focus on your breath. *Feel* and *see* everything that comes up in your mind. If you only have one minute before your children knock on the door, that's fine. My guess is you will have enjoyed that one brief moment. The next day, maybe you'll try to carve out a little more time for yourself. Meditation is like a self-fulfilling practice. The more you do it, the more you'll want to do it! So never worry about time. Just enjoy your little me-breaks throughout the forty days."

"Me-breaks—that sounds absolutely wonderful." Eve sighed in anticipation, uncurling her legs and stretching them out beside the fire.

Grace searched through the pile of driftwood, looking for a couple of larger pieces to add to the fire. "Consider meditation practice as the microcosm to the entire process of finding fulfillment, which is the macrocosm. In other words, in meditation practice, as well as in your journey toward fulfillment, do not focus on the obstacles, the negative. Do not focus on the time it takes to overcome them. Focus, instead, on the little moments where you feel good, and allow those to propel you forward into more and more and longer and longer moments of feeling good; that is the progression that moves us all forward along the path to fulfillment.

"If we imagine the path to fulfillment as a flight of stairs, the bottom of the staircase is analogous to us being asleep or unconscious. Our mind is controlled by the ego. Stuck in our knee-jerk reactions, thoughts and behaviours, we are just reliving our past, again and again, since we are unaware that there is a different way to live, a different way to be. We are unable to see a different perspective.

"To help clarify what I mean, here is an anecdote of how Columbus appeared to the Native Indians. The natives were at the seashore carrying out their daily activities. Some were washing, some were fishing; children were splashing and playing in the water, and the shaman of the village was looking out to sea. As the shaman scanned the horizon, he noticed a disturbance on the water. He could not discern what it was. It was as if, in a small section of water, the air broke into waves, similar to heat waves rising into the air from a hot surface. Every day he came back to watch the disturbance until several days had passed. Then one morning, as he studied the strange phenomenon, the waves suddenly coalesced into the shape of a tremendous ship. The shaman asked the people if they saw the great structure in the water, and as they stood on the shore searching the horizon, they each told him they did not. However, when the Shaman described exactly what he saw, putting the picture into their minds, piece by piece—the sails, the large wooden body, the ropes—the boat finally appeared to all."

How could they not see the ship? Eve wondered. *Am I just like the villagers, walking around unconscious, asleep?* She looked out toward the water, almost expecting to see Columbus's ship materialize out of thin air. "I really need a shaman," Eve acknowledged, "someone to help me see things more clearly."

"There have been many guides throughout our lifetimes showing us the steps to take on the path to fulfillment, great spiritual leaders or teachers, books and experiences, that have, like the shaman, shown us all a different perspective. And when we listen to their messages, we finally see that the world of limiting beliefs and the incessant, mental dissonance contributed by the ego's thoughts and views are only one way to live our lives. We learn that we can choose a different path—the path to a life of fulfillment and happiness. But if we do not know any other way to exist, we don't look for anything else. If we are unhappy but can't see a way out of it, we just resign ourselves to a life of unhappiness, and we wander through this beautiful landscape of life, seeing only suffering and pain. We are sleepwalking. We are unconscious and disengaged, removed from the passion and vibrancy of life."

Eve turned to look at the calm, serene face beside her. Pale orange firelight danced off Grace's soft features. *I wonder if Grace is my shaman,* she mused.

"As we make the choice to engage with life, to wake up and truly find our passion and vitality again, we take the first step on our path. The first step is the 'I *can't*' phase. 'I *can't* keep doing this'; 'I *can't* keep living like this.' This is a step up from being asleep. By perceiving that we are not happy, we acknowledge that we want more out of life than we are currently experiencing. As I pointed out earlier, this can be a very devastating stage for many of us because we become acutely aware of our suffering and are conscious of our pain. We may fall into the darkest of depressions, where we find ourselves at our absolute lowest—the very bottom of our entrenched ruts. But when we reach the bottom of our threshold for suffering, by finally saying, *'Enough is enough'* we can choose to overcome our complacency about tolerating our past tendencies and just enduring life. This phase then becomes a tremendous opportunity for change. If we hold onto the conviction that life can get better, that life is meant to be joyful, and that we are meant to be truly, unconditionally happy, then we can use the strength in that conviction to propel us up to the next step."

Eve broke off a small piece of driftwood, turning it between her fingers. "Well, I think I've finally reached the point where I can't keep doing this—this merry-go-round, this circus with Kathy and my parents." She threw the wood into the flames. "Enough certainly is enough!"

Grace smiled and continued. "Keep in mind, however, there is no timeline for walking the steps on our path. Without the knowledge of a different perspective, a different way to experience and live our lives, many people will remain at the bottom of the staircase, asleep for their entire physical existence. Others, perhaps, wake up just as they near the end of their physical lives. Some may find their way to the first step by realizing, with heart-wrenching sincerity, that they *'can't* keep doing this anymore!' But without a guide to show them any other way to live, to show them that they do have a choice, they may remain stuck in a dark, hopeless depression for weeks, months or even years. They will continue to dwell on their misery, talking and thinking about it incessantly, as they replay and relive their negative circumstances and feelings over and over again, which, as we have already discovered, is very counterproductive. This looping melancholy can keep us stuck in a very unhappy existence for an entire lifetime. Time is completely subjective and irrelevant on the path. The point is to *see*, to recognize the steps, and to make the choice to continue walking forward, focusing on *feeling good*—one baby step at a time. Each of those little baby steps are the actions and intentions we establish in order to climb out of our ruts and overcome our past tendencies and limiting beliefs. And each step is rooted in the unerring focus of feeling good.

"The next step on the path is the 'I *don't*' phase, where we make the powerful choice 'I *don't* want to do this anymore'; 'I *don't* want to feel like this any more.' This is a step of power. Even if we don't feel like we are being especially powerful, by just changing our wording we have moved from a phase of *inertia*—of only seeing and acknowledging our difficult life and the difficult situations and circumstances we are experiencing—into the realm of *action*. We make the commanding decision that *'enough is enough,'* and we set our intentions on climbing out of our ruts and our programmed tendencies! 'I *don't*,' by the way, is synonymous with 'I *can*.' 'I *can* do this.' 'I *can* change.' 'I *can* have the life I've always wanted.' 'I *can* be happy.'

"In this step, we start making some big changes in our lives. We make the choice to walk across the line, letting go of the pain and negative emotions associated with our past. Our body, mind and soul sit at the Round Table, listen to one another and find solutions that they can all agree upon. This is where we *fake it till we make it* and use affirmations to spur a change in our thought processes and behaviours. We use the SoS alert (the *Should* or *Shouldn't* alert) to help us recognize when we are falling back into our tribal beliefs. We focus on the simplicity of the waffle meter to help us discern which decisions and choices lead us toward happiness, by focusing on what is truly important in our lives, what truly feels good. As we focus on only wanting to feel good, we'll start making minor adjustments to our thoughts, words and actions. Focusing on things that will make us feel good throughout all areas of our lives—activities, environments, people and places—fosters a growing sense of ease and happiness. We focus on *I can* and *this feels good*. If we are really stuck and unsure of which activities or circumstances might best suit us, we need to focus on actions and thoughts that allow us to *feel better*. On the path, some changes we make may be small, where we focus on just *feeling better than we did before*, whereas other changes may be giant leaps of well-being as we catapult into feeling good. It is always a matter of making small baby steps upward. Every time we *feel better*, that pushes us toward feeling good."

Absently, Eve doodled in the sand with her finger while her thoughts wandered. It would be wonderful to always feel good, but she knew she had to deal with the parent and Kathy situations first. She'd already said, 'I can't do this any more,' so she just had to change her wording to 'I don't want to do this anymore'. She needed to stand her ground and choose actions that would pull her free of her ruts and preprogrammed tendencies. She needed to stand up for what she wanted—she needed to focus on her art and a harassment-free workplace. *Perhaps it really is that simple,* Eve conceded.

"Life really is simple," Grace continued, as if reading her mind. "We think it is complicated because the ego distracts us from what is truly important to our heart and our soul. It leads us away from what really makes us feel good and sends us on wild goose chases in search of material and financial acquisitions and status. It does not want to lose its identity and hold over us! So it will do everything within its power to make us falter on our path. It will throw handfuls of doubt, buckets of guilt and mountains of fear our way. As we move up the path to fulfillment, we must remember that enlightenment, or waking up, is a rather tumultuous stage of growth. In the game of life, these first couple of steps are similar to a rugby match. This is no gentlemen's sport! It can be downright dirty and hard. We may take two triumphant steps forward, only to fall face down as we struggle to overcome the firm grip of the ego's negative back talk, doubts, fears and limiting beliefs. However, if we doggedly persevere with our intention of *feeling good*, then we will find the fortitude to pick ourselves up once again, dust ourselves off and plough ahead. Then, as we focus on *feeling good*, making the necessary changes to our thoughts and in our lives, we will find our way to the next formidable step on the path—the 'I *won't*' phase, where we affirm, 'I *won't* feel like this ever again'; 'I *won't* compromise my authenticity'; 'I *won't* be held back any longer.' We will find that our body and mind surge with powerful energy, and we will feel a tremendous sense of well-being."

"I was just thinking that I don't want to do this anymore, this relentless game with Kathy and my parents. Now I guess I need to work on getting to the point where I *won't* do it anymore."

"Exactly, but be patient, Eve. Even when we get there, when we are living the good life on the third step of 'I won't,' life can throw us a curve ball. We may find ourselves experiencing negative thoughts and find we are right back in a situation we thought we had overcome. Recognize this as just a test and learn from it. Realize that we are back in the *feeling bad* space, and the alignment system is just letting us know we are falling into our old patterns and karmic cycles again. Acknowledge it and navigate back onto the path to fulfillment by focusing on feeling good and remembering our true wisdom—the knowledge of what is most important to us. If we do that, we will pass the test with flying colours.

Eventually, there will be no more tests, no more picking ourselves up and dusting ourselves off. We will remain at the top of the mountain, where the view is incredible."

Grace smiled. Stretching, she wrapped the blanket tighter around her legs. "This is the dawn of realization. This is truly the phase of unlimited potential, where we decide that for the rest of our magical journey, 'we *won't* compromise'! We focus on feeling good, and we vow to surround ourselves with the people and places that encourage and foster positive, happy thoughts and feelings; we chose to live our lives authentically. Authenticity is another step on the path to fulfillment." Grace paused. "Eve, how would you describe authenticity?"

Eve thought about that for a moment. *How do I describe authenticity?* Like a mother's soothing voice hushing her child into peaceful slumber, Eve could hear the wave's soft, rhythmic whisper—'shhh.' The night air was crisp and cool; a hint of fall hovered in the air. "This," she reasoned. "This experience, right now, right here, is authentic—enjoying the evening, the weather, the fire and your company." She looked over at Grace and smiled.

"So what is it about the experience that makes it authentic?" Grace questioned.

"I suppose because it feels right ... it feels good. I can't think of any place I'd rather be or anything else I'd rather be doing at this exact moment."

"Wonderful!" Grace beamed. "So if we focus on what *feels good* and what *feels right* or feels true to us, we will find our authenticity. Being authentic is about not compromising on our decision to feel good. It is about being honest with ourselves by listening openly and without judgment to our body and our mind. Like your observation, Eve, that nothing need be added or taken away from this evening's experience, that it's wonderful just the way it is. You feel good and you're happy. But being authentic is also about *expressing* that truth—feeling, acknowledging and honestly speaking what makes us happy, what *feels right* or true to us, in all areas of our lives. Being authentic means thinking, speaking and acting from a place of truth—from our inner truth—not from a *belief* based on other's influences, but a real, experiential, personal knowing."

"I want to be authentic, and I want to express my truth. But how can I? If I tell my parents that I *won't* go back to school, that I want to work on my art, I know it would just upset them. And then I'd have to sit and listen to the backlash. I'm not sure I can do that."

"If, for example, we are unhappy in a relationship, be it personal or working, and we hold in that unhappiness in an attempt to assuage conflict, whether it's due to uncertainty or fear of the consequences, then all we are doing is repressing our feelings, sweeping them under the rug and attempting to pretend that everything is okay. Being authentic is about acknowledging our feelings, no matter how uncomfortable or how inconvenient they are. Holding things in due to guilt, doubt, uncertainty or fear keeps us trapped in the ego and therefore stuck in suffering and unhappiness. We have to listen to our truth. No matter what discomfort is hiding behind those words and thoughts, we have to speak that truth. If we are unhappy with a situation, we have to speak the truth of it to ourselves, understand it, feel it. Then, if the situation deems it, we need to use compassion to express it. Often in relationships, when we express our feelings, the parties can work together to come up with a solution. Even if we are uncertain as to how our revelations will be received, we need to focus on being authentic, being true to how we feel and on feeling good. However, if we are not in a position to express outwardly how we are feeling because we are in an unsafe environment, then we must do whatever we can to find baby steps that will take us to a safer place and make us happier in the process.

"If we are in a marriage, for example, that is safe but we are unhappy, we need to honour that discomfort and examine just what it is that is making us unhappy. However, here's some food for thought. In today's society, it may seem easier to just walk away from a relationship that is unfulfilling rather than try to discern if our own thoughts or behaviours are the root causes of our unhappiness. Keep in mind that no matter where we go, or who we are with ... we always take *us* with us."

"I guess it's kind of like changing your socks. If your feet stink, changing your socks is probably not going to help all that much," Eve chuckled.

Grace laughed. "Exactly! So rather than jumping on board another bandwagon or getting different socks, we first need to look at our own house—our own behaviours and thought patterns. We need to determine if there is anything there that we can work on. Chances are, unless we are living through our soul and have completely transgressed the ego, there is plenty of work to do!

"Since we are looking at our own house, examining our own thoughts and behaviours, there's another interesting little nuance to relationships. Often, whenever someone rubs us the wrong way, irritates or upsets us, that person is only mirroring, or reflecting, our very own behaviour right back at us. Imagine a mime copying everything we do. In this case, whatever irritates or upsets us about the other person's behaviour is really just the universe's way of miming or shining a light on something we, ourselves, are doing in some area of our own lives. Say someone is very critical of us, nitpicking everything we do with annoying regularity. We need to contemplate if we might be doing the exact same thing, albeit in different circumstances or toward different people. Perhaps we are overly critical of our children or our parents or a friend. If someone gets a reaction out of us, pay attention and examine the source of that discomfort. We've already explored the concept that the alignment system uses discomfort to signal us to stop and pay attention to something in our thoughts or environment; this is just another possible motive. While it may be difficult to look upon someone else's questionable behaviour as a possible indicator of something we ourselves are doing, if we react to something someone has said or done, we need to shine that light back on our own behaviours so that we can discern whether or not there is a correlation there. Therefore, the next time we are bothered, be thankful. By drawing our attention back to our own behaviours, to our own house, we have been provided with a wonderful lesson."

I wonder if Kathy's nitpicking and belittling is the universe's way of mirroring my own behaviour back at me. Eve considered her relationships with her husband, her children, her friends and family. She didn't think there was a correlation there—in fact she was certain that she always went out of her way to make people feel accepted and worthy. She believed strongly in the adage, 'Do onto others as you would have them do onto you.' She didn't think she was overly critical, like Kathy was, but from now on, whenever her buttons got pushed, she would certainly look at each experience to make sure she wasn't engaging in that type of negative behaviour.

"Desire is another brilliant step on the path to fulfillment. Desire is essential to finding out what makes us tick, what makes us happy and feel good. But on the path, we have to realize that *our authentic truths* may not coincide with everyone else's desires and expectations. We have to be willing to stick to our guns, to honour our own unique desires and how we feel, because when we deny and repress our desires, we stifle our vibrancy. We diminish our spark, our passion, our very life force. Having desires is a wonderful thing—again, as long as we remember compassion. Our desires cannot hurt or harm another being, physically, emotionally or psychologically. When our desires are authentic and come from our higher self, we want to engage in what makes us feel good, and they drive us blissfully forward on the path to fulfillment. When we want something or want to do something, if we can afford it and it doesn't hurt anyone, then follow that desire. We need to find out what invigorates and enlivens us, find our passion again and incorporate it somehow into our lives. If we love to dance, take a dance class. If we love art, take classes or set time aside to create. If we love the outdoors, get out there and commune with nature. If skydiving invigorates us, take a leap of faith. Get turned on by life, Eve. Let it fuel you and impassion you. Always follow what makes you feel good!"

"You've helped me to realize and acknowledge just how important art is to me and how happy I feel when I am creating. I really need to incorporate it into my life. I need to set time aside to engage in those things that make me happy. I really need to take time for myself and what I love."

"It's absolutely essential to do what you love, Eve, to engage in those things that you are passionate about! And don't let others stop you from following that passion. Don't let their biases, opinions, judgments and limitations dictate what you do. Be compassionate but firm in your decisions. Be authentic. Do what makes you feel good."

Graced sorted through the dwindling pile of driftwood and placed two larger pieces onto the fire. The sudden surge of heat made Eve shuffle her bare legs a little further away from the flames.

"Nonjudgmental compassion is another step on the path. Can we truly see another being without the ego getting in the way? That is the objective of this step. We recognize that each person has her own unique background and her own unique past experiences; this menagerie of experiences and beliefs colours her views and opinions. But we also recognize that underneath all those layers of conditioning is a beautiful soul that just hasn't been heard. If someone is cruel or hateful toward us, we need to observe their behaviour and words without judgment. If we view others with nonjudgmental compassion, we can see that they can't help being anything but themselves; they are asleep, they do not know any other way. They haven't had the fortuitous experience of having a guide, whether in the form of a teacher, a book or an experience, open up their perception and show them a different way to live and be. They are stuck in their toxins and their assumptions. But we don't have to be affected by their behaviours, thoughts or words. If they are saying or doing something that is hurtful, we do not have to tolerate it; we can address their behaviour by expressing our truths and letting them know that their behaviour is unacceptable, or by expressing it to someone who has the authority to address their behaviour. If it is safe to do so, we can choose to simply walk away. *The key is to never take anything anyone ever says to us personally!* When they lash out, when they react, they are riding their wagon wheel, involved in their own world of suffering, their own disillusionment. It has nothing to do with us. So we can interact with them through compassion. Do not pass judgment on them, for they know not what they do. Let them carry on with their lives while we happily carry on with ours."

After all Kathy had said and done, Eve knew she was going to have a hard time viewing her in a nonjudgmental light. But she could start by refusing to let Kathy get to her.... Like Grace said, she could stop taking everything so personally. And if she were able to view the situation with compassion, then she would see Kathy for who she really was, a beautiful soul, still asleep and floundering around in the dark. She paused, marvelling at the clarity and logic of her astute observation. *Well, that certainly puts everything into a whole different perspective.*

Grace continued. "As we practise nonjudgmental compassion, we can begin to expand that sentiment by embodying pure, unconditional love. We need to extend an inclusive feeling of unconditional love to everyone and everything in our lives. Look upon everyone with love, whether they offer us challenges and obstacles to learn from or whether they are always loving and considerate to us. Do not restrict or qualify love. Feel love toward everyone, without censure. Give it a try. The Beatles said it very eloquently when they crooned, 'All you need is love.' Just imagine a boundless supply of love is available to us, and look upon everyone with love and gratitude. Everyone has a soul or essence or true nature, and we honour that soul by looking beyond everyone's outer expression of individuality, focusing instead on the beauty and love inside.

"If we take an empty plastic cup, an empty watering can and an empty champagne glass, we will have a lot of empty containers," Grace said, smiling. "Each container looks nothing like the other, but each is filled with the same substance—in this case, air. If we look beyond outer appearances, we will see that deep down inside, we are all of the same ilk. In fact, we are so interconnected that there is absolutely no separation at all. The fact that we think we are separate is one of the ego's most nefarious tricks. If we are all truly alone, then we must search constantly for meaning and fulfillment in our lives. Imagine how wonderful it would be to realize that we are never truly alone, that everything we do, think and say creates ripples in the ocean of life that affect everyone and everything. We are all together in this life experience. We just have to see through the ego's illusion. Picture a drop of water extracted from the ocean and placed into a glass decanter, which is then set to float upon the ocean. The drop of water, which is still the ocean, has no idea it is still connected since there is a glass shell separating it from the larger body of water. The ego is that shell. By filling us with limiting beliefs and distracting us from our true nature, ego creates a formidable boundary, resulting in us feeling alone. It is essential to realize that we are all drops from the same source of water. Our unique outer expressions have manifested in a medley of creative containers, but each of us, at our very core, is the same. We come from the same water; we are filled with the same substance—our soul or essence or true nature, which animates, enlivens and connects us to each other. It is essential to love everyone; for when we do, when we truly extend unconditional love outward, it reaches to the farthest heart and then comes back full circle to embrace our own.

"Viewing ourselves with non-judgment, love and compassion is just as important as viewing others without bias. It is often hard for us to *love* ourselves because we get caught up in our physical expressions. Our body is not *perfect*, we deduce, since it does not look like those airbrushed photographs in the magazines or like the *perfect* image we have in our own heads. It's easy to pick flaws in our appearance, and with an overactive ego it's also very easy to pick flaws in our personalities, our abilities and our confidence. Instead, focus on what's inside; then, with all the other steps we've taken and continue to take, we will love ourselves unconditionally."

Listening intently, Eve nodded. "It's kind of like the saying, 'Don't judge a book by its cover.' But very few people actually do that, myself included." She added honestly, "It's not easy to look beyond people's faults and foibles to see a beautiful soul underneath."

"Eve, I want you to imagine a playground, with swings and slides, that is empty save for a small child around two or three years old. She is crying. In fact, she is outright sobbing, standing alone in the sand. You look around for a parent or caregiver, but there is no one there … just this very tiny, very upset child. Her cheeks are wet with the tears streaming down from her frightened eyes. She is looking helplessly around for someone, anyone, to tell her everything is going to be okay, but she has been left painfully alone. There is no one near to hold her and reassure her. You look around desperately for someone to come soothe the child. Failing to find anyone, you walk over and try to speak with her. Her sobs are heart-wrenching. You squat down so that you can talk to her, and you ask her if she is hurt. She shakes her head no. You ask if someone is nearby, her mommy or her daddy, or perhaps a babysitter or relative to look after her. Again she shakes her head no. You stand up, and she grabs hold of your leg and starts to cry even harder. You pick her up and sit on a nearby bench. Slowly, you begin to rock back and forth as you whisper soothing words into her ears. You tell her everything is going to be okay, everything is going to be all right. She looks up at you through hiccupping tears, and she says, 'I bad.' Startled, you look down at this tiny child and wonder what on earth she could have done to believe that she is bad. You tell her that no, she is not bad, but she just wails harder against your shoulder and cries out, 'I bad! I bad!' Now what if you realized that this little girl is you? That this little girl has been locked inside your heart, arms outstretched, tears falling silently for years, waiting for you to tell her everything is going to be okay, that she is not a bad girl.

"She cries and tells you all the negative things you've said to yourself and have been told by others. She tells you how weak she is, how ugly she is. How stupid she is. That she is useless and worthless. She shakes with the effort of her tears as she repeats over and over again that she is bad. Stricken, you tell her that she is a wonderful, smart, beautiful, lovely, good little girl. You tell her you love her. She looks up into your eyes and her tears begin to slow. She has been waiting so very long for this moment when you finally hold her and tell her, from the boundlessness of your heart, that you love her, that she is worthy and deserving of your love, that your love is unconditional and that you love her for who she is and the beautiful woman she's become."

Eve, touched deeply by that story, sniffed audibly. A single tear escaped, rolling down her cheek, leaving a shimmering trail in the pale firelight. "I know I've had a difficult time trying to love myself unconditionally. I know that throughout my life I've been very hard on myself. I've continuously berated myself, repeatedly focusing on the negative, but I think I'm finally beginning to understand how to accept myself now. Thank you."

"You're most welcome, Eve." Grace smiled. "And I'm especially happy you expressed that sentiment with sincere thankfulness, since gratitude is another wonderful step on the path to fulfillment. Focusing on anything and everything we can think of to be grateful for is a powerful way to propel us toward happiness and fulfillment. Too often we focus on lack, lamenting what we do not have, rather than celebrating the blessings and treasures that are already here for us, right now at this moment. We need to foster an appreciation for all the good that is already present in our lives and then give thanks for its manifestation into our experience. Admittedly, this can sometimes seem harder than it sounds, since we tend to dwell on the glass being half empty. If we are having a particularly rough time as we work our way toward happiness, being thankful for the little things in life, like a cup of tea or a pillow to rest our heads on, is much better than focusing on losing our jobs or falling out of a relationship. The point is to remain positive.

"It's extremely easy to focus on the negative. Which is why as we progress on the path, it is essential to recognize and move beyond the 'but, but, but' arguments that the ego tries to thwart us with. We try hard to find things to be grateful for; we make an effort to rediscover our desires, and we try to look at others without judgment. 'But,' the ego says …. 'But I lost my job, I can't afford a cup of tea'; 'but I don't have time to meditate, I'm too exhausted by the time I get the kids into bed'; 'but I'm too overwhelmed, I don't have time to play in the garden, I have real concerns'; 'but she said I was bossy.' But *is one of the ego's favourite words, keeping us locked in a vicious cycle of excuses* not *to feel good*. Realize this! Recognize when we are making excuses! We must not let the ego's devious diversions lure us away from the path. We need to stay the course and focus on the positive. And what better way to focus on feeling good than to recognize what we already have in our lives that is making us happy and allowing us to feel good right now. What we think and what we feel attracts more of the same. If we focus on what feels good, we will bring more things into our experience that will make us feel good. Conversely, if we feel bad, we just attract more reasons to continue to feel bad.

"Gratitude works the same way, except that it adds a kind of double whammy, so to speak, since *what we are grateful for, we have already manifested or brought into our experience.* How's that for a motivator? Our past thoughts and desires have already brought wonderful experiences into our lives. We already have things, right here and now, that are making us feel good. Like I mentioned earlier, the thoughts we had yesterday create our today, and the thoughts we have today create our tomorrow. Appreciate that—because of some *feel good* thoughts that we had *yesterday*, we've already created some wonderful experiences that are now present in our lives *today*. Then, for the duration of the day, continue to focus on creating and maintaining more positive thoughts so that we'll experience a positive, bright, happy tomorrow," Grace said and smiled. "And a positive, bright, happy tomorrow is definitely something to be grateful for!"

"It sure is," Eve said, agreeing wholeheartedly with Grace. It was time for her to start creating that bright, happy future, to stop hiding in the shadows of other people's expectations and beliefs and finally let herself shine. It was time to embrace her truth. She felt a sense of lightness envelop her.

The fire was dying. The wood, black and charred, had collapsed into the pit, where orange embers pulsed. The forest was a wall of darkness behind her. Beyond the faint glow from the hot embers, the beach disappeared around them, merging into the depths of the lake as the water blurred into the obsidian sky. Eve may not be able to see what her future held, but by focusing on what felt good, right here and now, it was only a matter of time before the future started to resemble her new positive outlook, her new brighter perspective.

"I have a proposition for you, Eve. Every day, before you retire for the night or the moment you wake up, I want you to get into the habit of saying five things for which you are grateful. It can even become a part of your meditation. Close your practice with, 'I am grateful for …' and list five things, no matter how small or how insignificant they may seem. By practising gratitude you start a gratitude bank, where every deposit compounds over time. Soon, you will experience a life of overflowing gratitude and overflowing abundance!"

"Just five things?" Eve considered. "That seems easy enough. I can think of five right off the top—my wonderful husband, Tom; my two beautiful children; our health; this magnificent day; and, of course, meeting you, Grace." Eve smiled from ear to ear.

"I'm honoured to be a part of your list." Grace returned Eve's smile with a radiant grin of her own. "Thank you."

Chapter 11

Footprints in the Sand

Eve picked out a skinny stick from the few remaining bits and pieces of driftwood and nudged the embers at their feet. Tossing in a few small chunks of wood, she watched as the flames momentarily surged back to life. "I'm grateful for a chance to enjoy something as simple as our little campfire."

Grace shifted and curled her legs beneath her. "We can find lots of things in our lives to be grateful for. The only challenging part is recognizing them, becoming aware of what we've already got. And that, Eve, is the first of five really important concepts to keep in mind as you climb the path to fulfillment.

"As we climb upward on the path, five concepts guide each step we take—awareness, perception, choice, wisdom and detachment. We've actually already discussed these concepts in detail today."

Eve interrupted. "Honestly, Grace, we've discussed a lot today. I'm not sure I can recall when we spoke about these concepts directly. I know you've mentioned choice a lot, and I understand wisdom, but I can't remember exactly what awareness and perception are." She paused, knitting her eyebrows together. "I don't recall hearing about detachment, though."

Grace smiled. "The reason why you don't recall detachment is because I haven't actually labelled it as such yet. But before I explain it to you, let me refresh your memory, since we have talked about a great deal today.

"Awareness is the guide that illuminates the path. It is the force that dissolves our perceived limitations. With awareness, we wake up. We begin to become *aware* of our role in creating a life of happiness, and we become *aware* of the steps necessary to manifest it.

"You became *aware* of your soul, Eve, and the role the ego plays in your life when you placed all your labels, masks and hats into the shoebox. You discovered that you could create your tomorrow by changing your thoughts today. You examined the SOS alert and realized that by saying *should* or *shouldn't* you were pulled back into your tribal beliefs. You became aware of your truths, your authenticity, how you like your eggs—removed from everyone else's expectations, biases or opinions. You explored your patterns and karmic cycles, and you became *aware* of your biggest ruts. Then you learned that in order to find happiness and fulfillment, you needed to follow your passion by focusing on what makes you feel good, even if it doesn't correspond to everyone else's expectations.

"When you became aware, you woke up, and your perception broadened. You began to see your life differently. You recognized the difference between living in the calm hub of the wheel and living on the chaotic outer rim, subject to life's ups and downs. You saw how the ego, with its shadow self and burden body, restricted your ability to find lasting happiness by filling you with limiting beliefs and distracting you from what really matters in your life. You saw how the past was holding you back, and you experienced a fundamental change in perception when you let the past go.

"We all interact with life based on our own unique perceptions. If we feel restricted and we think our life is limited, it will be—after all, that's how we see it. But that is just one way of looking at it. If we decide to change our perception and instead see a life of promise and opportunity, we can use the 'fake it till you make it' approach and enlist the aid of affirmations to turn life around to reflect our way of thinking. It's all just a matter of perspective. It all boils down to choice.

"And as you mentioned, I have spoken a lot about choice today because it is essential to realize that you always have a choice in how you think, speak and act. If you are not happy, choose to think, speak and act differently. Choose to feel good. Choose to follow what's important in your life. Choose to be authentic. And once you make those choices, do not compromise!

"I know the concept of wisdom really resonated with you, Eve. Wisdom is all about discerning what it is that makes you happy or what feels good. It is the knowledge of what is truly important to you. Is it love or empty material possessions and status that are important? Is it the quality or the quantity in life that is motivating your actions? What is it that is most important to you? When you discover the answers to that inquiry, you will be able to use those revelations to guide you unerringly toward fulfillment. This is where the waffle meter and the alignment system come in. Realize that when we feel stress or unease or find ourselves stuck in another rut or reacting when another one of our triggers is pressed, it is the alignment system pointing the way to happiness. We need to recognize and feel the discomfort and then use the waffle meter to help inform us about which path to choose. If it feels bad, we are off track and following a path that will only lead to more opportunities to feel bad. Use the tools available to you, Eve, and always, without fail, choose the path of feeling good."

"I will definitely use all the tools you've given me on my path to feeling good." Eve paused. "But you still haven't explained detachment."

"Detachment is the art of letting go. We've actually spoken quite a lot about letting things go, but I've held off using the term *detachment* until now because detachment is a very misunderstood concept. When people think of detachment, they think of being insensitive, cold or emotionally void—a kind of numb, nonchalant, indifferent attitude, where we walk around and interact with people projecting an image of being aloof and uncaring. That is not the detachment I want you to embrace, Eve. Detachment comes when we stop fighting the flow of life——when we no longer *react* to everything that gets thrown our way *but accept it and move on*. 'It is what it is' is a valuable statement to embrace, in that it always *is* just *what it is*. The problem is not that life is the way it is and that things constantly happen and inevitably change; the problem lies in the quandary that we have a particularly troublesome habit of pinning the labels *good* or *bad* to life. Without that label or categorization of things, events and circumstances, things are just things, events are just events, and circumstances are just circumstances. We may not want to dwell on them or experience them for long, but if we remove the label of *good* or *bad*, they are really just what they are, another set of lessons and experiences. Don't get caught up in the label game. Move toward feeling better if you are not happy. Do your best to create actions that will lead you toward fulfillment. Change your attitude and your behaviours by following what feels good, and release the counterproductive impulse to label everything.

"Expectations are just labels we project into the future and they are, equally, a recipe for disaster. When we tell ourselves, 'Oh, it will be so good if *this* happens,' the consequence of this type of thinking is that if it *doesn't* happen, we will *not* feel good. And if it does happen, wonderful! We'll be happy for a moment, until, of course, the next time life doesn't live up to our expectations. Our expectations have us riding on the outside rim of the wheel, just reacting to life. When it's good, we are up; when it's bad, we are down. It's as simple as that. In order to find lasting happiness and fulfillment, we need to get off that crazy ride. We need to let go of expectations. When we can truly accept that concept, thereby releasing our need to control everyone and everything, we are finally able to relax and find some peace! What an awful lot of effort and energy it has taken all these years to try to control our lives. Let it go. See what happens. Have fun and just roll with it.

"Another aspect of detachment is the ability to be like water off a duck's back. Let everything negative that anyone ever says to us just slide off. Don't let it attach; don't let it take hold. Just let it go. Do not take anything personally … ever, no matter what—no ifs, ands, or buts!"

Eve thought about that. "I recognize that in certain situations in the past, I've jumped to conclusions and taken things personally. But you've shown me how limiting that can be, how much stress it can cause—both emotionally and physically. I need to let things go, to stop reacting and start accepting things just as they are and move forward."

"To move forward, though, we also need to have a certain level of detachment when we are standing up for ourselves and expressing *our* needs and *our* desires. We have to understand that, since everyone else is looking at us through their own filters and sunglasses, they may not appreciate our views and decisions. We have to let that go and not allow their reactions or opinions to suppress our passion and our inner light. This is not about being insensitive and uncaring to their fears and concerns. We need to be compassionate and empathetic as we express ourselves, but we have to stand by our conviction to be authentic and follow what makes us happy. Above all else, Eve, to thine own self be true. Always do what makes you happy."

Leaning toward the fire, Grace angled her watch into the light. "It's getting quite late." She walked over to the lake's edge and filled her thermos with some water. Returning, she doused the few remaining embers. Walking back to the shore one last time to refill her thermos, she emptied that on the ashes too, just for good measure. Eve watched silently.

Grace stood waiting patiently as Eve slowly got to her feet. They walked back to the deck in silence. Their chairs were still there, lit vividly by bright Chinese lanterns that hung between the posts that marked the four corners of the deck. Their time together was quickly coming to a close. What could Eve possibly say to this woman to express how grateful she was that they had met and how blessed she felt to have had this time with her? They walked up onto the deck. "Grace, I don't know how to thank you … for everything." Eve faltered.

Grace gave Eve a warm hug. "You don't have to thank me for anything. It was my pleasure."

"But I do," Eve insisted. She drew back from Grace's embrace and searched her face. *Can eyes truly convey the amount of love and gratitude a person can feel?* Eve wondered. She hoped so, since there was just no way to put into words how much this day meant to her. "You've changed my life." Eve spoke softly. "You've taught me so much. I've learned so much about myself and my tendencies. You've shown me how to look within myself for true happiness. I can honestly say that I now see that I have an unlimited capacity for peace and joy. I am extremely grateful to you for your wisdom and your selflessness. Grace, you've spent an entire day helping me sort through my baggage and my problems. Because of you, my tomorrow will be different. My life will be different." She added, "I am different."

Stricken with a sudden thought, Eve glanced at Grace in concern. "What if I have more questions? What if I can't remember everything? How can I find you? Surely we can keep in touch."

Grace smiled. "You have everything you need to be truly happy, Eve, you always have. It has just been a matter of remembering your potential. And I think you've done that." Grace gave Eve's hand a gentle, reassuring squeeze. "You are whole and perfect just the way you are. Nothing needs to be added; you've been ready for happiness and fulfillment since the moment you were born. It's time to take your first step back onto that path. But if you need me, Eve, I'll never be far away."

As Eve was about to delve into that cryptic message, the phone in her pocket vibrated. She reached down and looked at the number; it was Tom. Looking at the time on her cell phone, she realized Tom must be worried about her. She turned to Grace. "I'll just be a moment. It's Tom."

"Hi, honey. No, everything's okay. I've just been hanging around the beach all day, talking." Eve smiled at Grace and then turned and looked down into the water. She could see Grace's reflection smiling back at her. "How was the fishing?" She listened intently, her gaze drifting out over the dark, inky water. Her children, awake well past their bedtime, each popped onto the phone to tell her about their prize catches of the day. Her youngest regaled her with the heroic, bloody tale of how a fishing hook got caught in his thumb and how Daddy had to remove it with some pliers. After receiving first aid, the thumb was as good as new, and he couldn't wait to show her his wound. She smiled and listened patiently. When Tom came back on the phone, she let him know that she'd arrive shortly. She just had to say good-bye to her new friend. She closed her phone and returned it to her pocket. She turned around to acknowledge her friend, but Grace was nowhere to be seen. She scanned the beach, but there was absolutely no sign of her. Eve called out her name several times, but there was no answer.

Where is she? Where did she go? Confused, Eve just stood there. *How can she just disappear into thin air?*

Stop looking out there for answers. Grace's voice echoed inside her. *I'm right here ... I always have been, and I always will be.*

Eve paused as realization dawned. *Is it possible?* She thought about Grace's reflection smiling back at her. *Could it really be ...?*

Stepping off the deck with starlight guiding her, Eve made her way back toward the chalet. After a few steps, she noticed footprints leading to the deck from the area where she and Grace had been sitting, enjoying the warmth of the fire. She smiled. There was only one set of footprints in the sand.

About the Authors

Annemarie is a mixed media and collage artist and former elementary school teacher whose lifelong passion for art has continued into her recent retirement. Since then, her other passion, yoga, has emerged as a second career. Annemarie became a registered yoga instructor and opened Annemarie's Yoga Studio. Annemarie has two amazing grown children, Tyler and Amber. She lives in Oshawa, Ontario, Canada, with her remarkable artist husband, Gary, and their delightful cat, Mutzi.

Marissa is a freelance writer and has been dedicated to expressing herself through the written word since she was old enough to hold a crayon. Marissa is a registered yoga instructor and offers classes out of her studio, Pure Intention Yoga in Brooklin, Ontario, Canada. Marissa lives in Brooklin with her wonderful husband, David, three handsome sons, Lochlin, Aidan and Brendan, two adorable dogs, Razz and Michaella, and two companionable fish, Neo and Dalmatian Fishy.

For Annemarie and Marissa, writing *LIFE* is the culmination of an entire lifetime of introspection and reflection. Through their passion to reach out and help others, they realized the urgent need for this very relevant and timely book.

May you each find the LIFE you've always wanted!

In gratitude,

Annemarie & Marissa

We would love to hear from you! If you enjoyed the book or found its message helpful and meaningful to you, we would love to hear your stories!

Annemarie Greenwood:
annemaries.yoga@sympatico.ca
www.annemariesyoga.ca

Marissa Campbell:
marissa@pureintention.ca
www.pureintention.ca

CPSIA information can be obtained at www.ICGtesting.com
Printed in the USA
LVOW101954130212

268510LV00004B/6/P